Principles of Microeconomics

By

Pirudas L. Lwamugira

authorHOUSE

1663 LIBERTY DRIVE, SUITE 200
BLOOMINGTON, INDIANA 47403
(800) 839-8640
www.authorhouse.com

First published by AuthorHouse 08/23/04

ISBN: 1-4184-8269-2 (sc)

Library of Congress Control Number: 2004094921

Printed in the United States of America
Bloomington, Indiana

This book is printed on acid-free paper.

Cover photo courtesy of Fitchburg State College.

For Emelda, Lillian, Jeremy and David
Thank you for your support

TABLE OF CONTENTS:

PREFACE

The purpose of this book, like the Principles of Macroeconomics counterpart, is to provide instructors and students a concise text that covers the core principles of macroeconomics that can be taught in a semester. This is done without sacrificing the content or the rigorous examination of macroeconomic theory. It deliberately avoids overwhelming students with information overload. The book does not seek to make economics interesting, entertaining, or 'simple'. It simply encourages the mastery and application of the basic macroeconomic principles, and the development of critical thinking. It emphasizes the mastery of the basic economic principles by repeating explanations and definitions of certain economic concepts like economic efficiency, a change in demand versus a change in quantity demanded and by placing an emphasis on problem solving. In some cases synonyms of certain words are provided. Do not, therefore, be surprised by the repetitive nature of the book because the motto is to 'leave no student behind'. The content and structure of the book should benefit students who go on to do advanced work in economics as well as those who just take one economics course and stop at that.

The main distinguishing characteristic of this book is its structure. I have always subscribed to the philosophy of a certain great educator (I cannot remember his name) who said that 'you can teach anything to anybody as long as it is well structured'. This has been the guiding principle in my teaching and in writing this book.

The instructor who emphasizes class discussions and encourages students to discover for themselves the meanings and applications of certain economic concepts will find this book particularly useful. Few application examples are given and everything is left to the instructor and the students to come up with their own examples. That way, the students are encouraged to pose and think about the issues rather than read the examples in the book and move on. In any case, macroeconomic and microeconomic issues change rapidly so everybody is better off discussing current economic issues.

As much as possible debate and personal opinions on various economic issues are avoided. Government price controls, for example, provide an opportunity for a lively classroom discussion, but in this text they are discussed in the context of applying the competitive market model and a detailed analysis of the pros and cons of these controls are left to the instructor.

Homework problems are provided at the end of some chapters and again the idea is to encourage students to apply economic concepts, think critically, write about economic issues, and develop problem-solving skills. To that end, multiple-choice questions are avoided and there is no test-bank. It is left to the instructor to design tests that will give a proper feedback on the understanding and application of the course material covered.

ACKNOWLEDGMENTS

I would like to thank my economics professors at Temple University who taught me economics and my Fitchburg State College colleagues Dr. Carolyn Murphy, Dr. Michael Turk and Dr. Nancy Wiegersma whose numerous exchanges on teaching economics enhanced my teaching abilities. The same heart felt gratitude is also extended to my former colleagues at La Salle University in Philadelphia from whom I learned a lot. Special thanks go to Dr. Michael Turk who edited and reviewed the contents of this book. I would also like to thank Dr. Gerald Higdon of the Mathematics department at Fitchburg State College who helped me with some of the mathematical functions used in the book.

Lastly, I would like to thank all the students I have taught over time. My interactions with them have given me a wonderful learning experience about the art of teaching in general and the methods of teaching economics in particular.
I would particularly like to thank my students at Fitchburg State College who were intimately involved in helping with this project. Besides acting as guinea pigs for the homework assignments, my students were a useful resource for class testing the manuscript. Some students reviewed and edited the manuscript and provided feedback for which I am very grateful. In this regard, the following students deserve special mention: Kimberly Waynelovich, Jennifer Fitchner, Heather Bell, Adam Gelinas, Gregory Duclos, Donald Roberts, Tanya Arndt, Alyssa Morand, Tammy Cormier, Paula DeLisle, Paul LeBlanc, Elise Kimball, Kelly deBoer, Joshua Hertel, Amy Dean, and Julie-Ann Keane.
The errors and omissions found in this book are my sole responsibility.

Please direct your comments to:
plwamugira@fsc.edu

CHAPTER 1: THE BASIC ECONOMIC PROBLEM (SCARCITY AND CHOICE)

Economics is the study of how **scarce** resources are allocated among **competing** wants. In other words, economics deals with what economists call the Basic Economic Problem. The basic economic problem is simply that while peoples' wants are unlimited, the resources to satisfy these wants are limited. The key words in the definition of economics are 'scarce resources' and 'competing wants.' This is a problem because the scarce resources, which have alternative uses, must be allocated in such a way that most of the unlimited wants are satisfied. Every country, rich or poor, is confronted with this problem.

Economics tries to deal with the basic economic problem by addressing three basic questions namely; What? How?, and For Whom? Since human needs are for goods and services, society must determine **what** goods and services to produce. This question deals with the problem of output selection or the allocation problem. As long as resources are limited, and have many alternative uses, there should be a mechanism that determines to which of the many uses the resources will be allocated.

Let us use the classical guns versus butter argument to explain the above problem. We may all agree that every country needs some form of national defense but at the same time the basic needs for food, shelter and clothing must also be satisfied. Given our limited resources, how much should be allocated to national defense and how much should be allocated to the basic needs? There is always spirited debate on this problem whenever politicians and other policy makers try to resolve it. How much should be allocated to the production of health care services? How much should be allocated to education, housing, cars, buses, and refrigerators? In output selection we must decide how much we want to produce. Suppose we decide to produce, as is normally the case, a combination of goods. In our case we have decided that defense is necessary but so is butter. The next problem is to determine the proportions in which goods and services should be produced. Once that problem is settled, we must decide whether we want to produce these goods and services now or in the future. In determining how much we want to produce and the proportions and the time in which to produce them, we have to make choices. We are forced to make choices because resources are limited! This is the reason why economics is sometimes referred to as the science of choice.

After we have somehow determined what to produce, we must decide **how** production will take place. This is called production planning. Again since resources are limited, we are required to combine factors of production (resources) namely labor, capital, land and entrepreneurship to get the maximum output out of these resources.

Labor is the combination of peoples' physical and mental capabilities that can be used in producing goods and services. Capital (investment goods) is people-made means of production that include; machines, equipment, plants, and other facilities that are used to produce goods and services. Land refers to all natural resources or gifts of nature such as; forests, arable land, rivers, oceans, lakes, and mineral deposits that are used in the production of goods and services.

Entrepreneurship refers to the special ability to innovate, take risks, organize resources, and make basic business decisions that determine the successes of a business.

If, for example, we decide to use labor and capital in our production process, we must still determine the proportions in which these factors are to be combined. Should factor proportions be biased in favor of labor or capital? If factor proportions are biased in favor of labor (meaning more proportions of labor are used than those of capital), then a labor-intensive mode of production is used. If factors of production are biased in favor of capital, a capital-intensive mode of production is used. We still have to face the question of choice even in production planning. It is imperative that our resources be used efficiently. We must strive to achieve what is called production (engineering) efficiency and allocation (economic) efficiency. Production efficiency is achieved when a given level of resources and technology give us the maximum level of output. In other words we produce at the lowest possible cost. Allocative or economic efficiency is achieved when marginal cost is equal to price (P = MC), i.e. when the marginal valuation of the product by consumers is equal the opportunity cost of producing that product[1] *(This important relationship will be explained later in chapter8)* Production efficiency and economic efficiency guarantee us the largest possible production of goods and services that our resources can possibly produce to satisfy our wants at a fair price.

After we have resolved the problems of output selection and production planning, we must determine how the output produced is to be distributed among consumers. **For whom** have we produced? This is the distribution question. Our aim, in this case, is to determine who gets what and in what amounts. A nation has now baked a very large cake (the national output) and we have to determine who receives a slice of this cake and the sizes of the slices. The distribution question also implies choice. In short, the basic economic problem is the problem of 'scarcity and choice.'

We have to make choices because our resources are limited. Every time we make choices, it means some wants and needs are left unmet. We cannot have everything we want. Why? The problem of choice leads us to an important concept of 'opportunity cost.' The opportunity cost of a particular action is the next best alternative that is not chosen. Put differently, the opportunity cost of any decision is the highest valued next best alternative that must be sacrificed to satisfy a want. If say you choose to go to school full time the opportunity cost of going to school would be the wages that you forgo. Suppose you had some money that you can use either to repair your car on use it for a vacation. If you decide to repair your car instead of going on vacation the opportunity cost of repairing your car is the loss of a vacation. Opportunity cost is a very important concept in economics because economic decisions are evaluated by using this concept. Resources will flow from one economic sector to another based on the opportunity cost of resource use.

---

[1] The concept of economic efficiency is explored in detail in chapter 6

The following production possibilities table demonstrates the opportunity cost concept:

THE PRODUCTION POSSIBILITIES TABLE				
			COST OF WHEAT IN TERMS OF CORN (CORN GIVEN UP)	
	BUSHELS OF WHEAT	BUSHELS OF CORN	WHEAT INCREMENTS	TOTAL COST	COST PER ONE BUSHEL OF WHEAT
A	0	90			
B	10	85	1st 10	5	10:5=1:0.5
C	20	75	2nd 10	10	10:10=1:1
D	30	60	3rd 10	15	10:15=1:1.5
E	40	40	4th 10	20	10:20=1:2
F	50	0	5th 10	40	10:40=1:4

Let us suppose that a farmer with limited land (about three acres) has one tractor and two helpers to use on her farm. If she allocates **all** her resources to the production of corn, she will produce ninety bushels of corn and zero bushels of wheat. If she were to decide to produce both wheat and corn, then some resources will have to be moved from corn production to wheat production and in the process the production of wheat will decline. In the above table we can see that as the production of wheat is increased from zero to ten, the corn output falls from ninety bushels to eighty-five. The opportunity cost of producing ten units of wheat is the loss of five units of corn. The trade off is one to one half. That is for every unit of wheat produced, one half unit of corn is given up on the average. Note that, on account of limited resources, it is impossible to produce ninety units of corn and any amount of wheat. Any subsequent combination of wheat and corn, after the first combination, must lead to a loss in corn. Note also from the table that the more we produce the greater the opportunity cost. This is the so-called law of increasing costs. The opportunity cost increases from five to ten, ten to fifteen and so on. On the average, the cost of one unit of wheat produced increases from a half to one, from one to one and half and so on. The Principle of Increasing Costs arises because resources tend to be fixed and specific. Since resources are fixed and specific (specialized) an allocation from where they are more productive (more suited) to where they are less productive, will lead to higher opportunity costs.

The information shown on the table above can also be shown with a graph called the Production Possibilities Curve or the Production Possibilities Frontier or the Transformation Curve. The graph below shows what it would mean, in terms of resource allocation, if you produced on the production possibilities curve, outside the production possibilities, or inside the production possibilities.

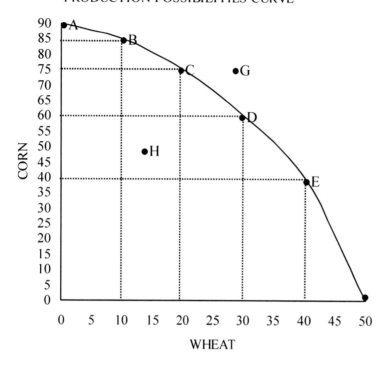

PRODUCTION POSSIBILITIES CURVE

A to F ---------------------- Efficient points (efficient resource allocation
                                    or full employment)
H ------------------------------ Inefficient resource allocation (underemployment)
G ------------------------------ Unattainable (not feasible)
A ------------------------------ All corn and no wheat
F ------------------------------ All wheat and no corn

When there is a quantitative or a qualitative increase in resources, more goods and services will be produced. In our example of wheat and corn production, it would mean more of these two products would be produced. We now have more goods or more possibilities in terms of the goods we can have. In this case the production possibilities curve will shift outward. Instead of using wheat and corn as an example, we can use capital goods on one hand and consumer goods on the other to make general observations about the whole economy. Capital goods or investment goods are things like machines, factories, and new buildings that are used to produce future goods and services. Consumer goods are things that are available for consumption now and do not contribute to the future production of goods and services. At full employment, we will have the maximum of capital goods and consumer goods being produced. An outward shift in the production possibilities curve of capital goods and consumer goods will mean that more capital goods and consumer goods are being produced than before and this will indicate economic growth. Economic growth is so basic because more and better goods and services should be produced to provide for an increasing population and provide a higher standard of living for everyone.

A SHIFT IN THE PRODUCTION POSSIBILITIES CURVE AS A RESULT OF AN INCREASE IN RESOURCES OR AN IMPROVEMENT IN TECHNOLOGY FOR PRODUCING BOTH WHEAT AND CORN

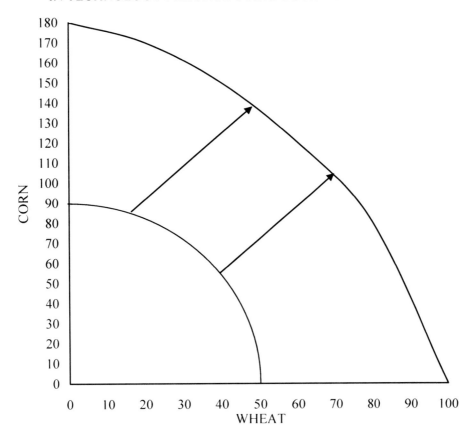

A SHIFT IN THE PRODUCTION POSSIBILITIES CURVE AS A RESULT OF A DECREASE IN RESOURCES OR A DECLINE IN TECHNOLOGY FOR PRODUCING BOTH WHEAT AND CORN

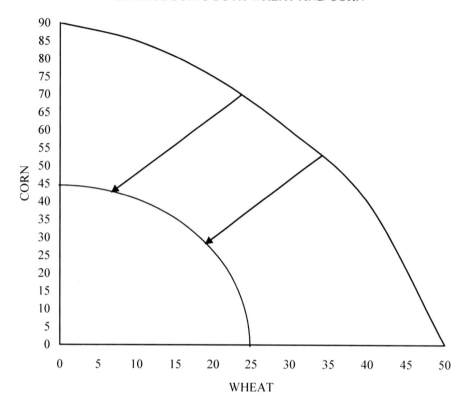

CHANGE IN THE PRODUCTION POSSIBILITIES CURVE AS A RESULT OF AN INCREASE IN RESOURCES FOR PRODUCING CORN OR AN IMPROVEMENT IN TECHNOLOGY FOR PRODUCING CORN

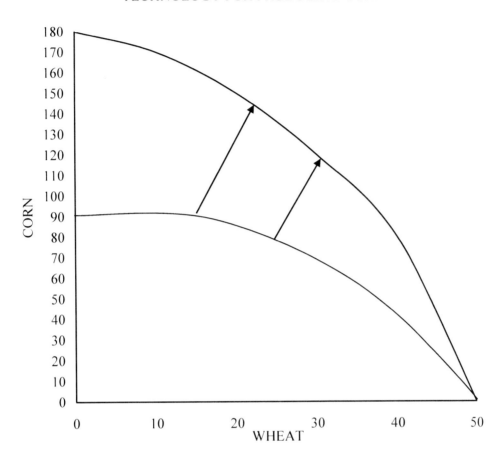

A CHANGE IN THE PRODUCTION POSSIBILITIES CURVE AS A RESULT OF AN INCREASE IN RESOURCES FOR PRODUCING WHEAT OR AN IMPROVEMENT IN TECHNOLOGY FOR PRODUCING WHEAT

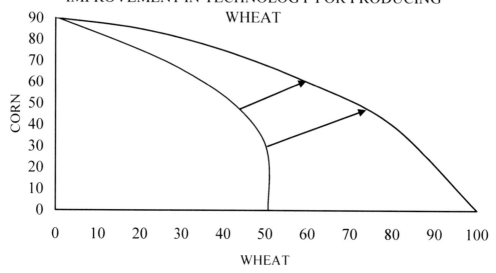

An economic system must perform four important tasks. It must determine the composition of the national output, allocate resources, distribute the output and provide economic growth. The most important point that we should now discuss is the mechanism through which these functions are carried out. In a planned economy, as was the case in the Soviet Union, some central authority will attempt to determine what and how much the factories will produce, how much resources will be allocated to them and how the product will be distributed. In a free market economy with no central authority, all these four important functions are carried out by the price system also known as the free market system. The price system is a system where resources are allocated through the forces of supply and demand.

Economic terms to remember:

The basic economic problem	Production possibilities curve
The law of increasing costs	Opportunity cost
Economic efficiency	Production efficiency
Production possibilities table	Factors of production
Labor	Land
Capital	Entrepreneurship

CHAPTER 2: THE FREE MARKET SYSTEM

In 1776, a British philosopher named Adam Smith published a treatise titled, 'An Inquiry into the Causes of the Wealth of Nations'. Adam Smith's treatise was published in a historically important book known as the Wealth of Nations. During that time, the prevailing economic and political view was that government officials were the best judges in determining what was best for the individual. Smith argued that it was the individual workers and producers, interested only in helping themselves, that were responsible for the increase in the economic well being of themselves and others. In the process of pursuing their own self-interest, individuals would further the public interest. Smith asserted that a system of individual liberty provided the best opportunities for individuals to create wealth for themselves and in the process create wealth for others. He used the analogy of an 'invisible hand' to describe how, without any formal coordination, buyers and sellers would reach a desirable social outcome as if guided by an invisible hand. Smith's free market system is studied by using the Competitive Equilibrium Market Model.

THE COMPETITIVE EQUILIBRIUM MARKET MODEL: SUPPLY AND DEMAND

Economists use the competitive equilibrium market model to describe the economic outcomes of consumer and producer interaction in a free market economy. Economic models are simplifications of real life situations that are designed to simplify reality and make real world events easier to understand. Consumers and producers interact in the market guided by different motives. Consumers will try to maximize their satisfaction (utility) and producers will try to maximize profits[2]

Utility is the satisfaction a consumer gets from the consumption of a product. It is generally accepted that as more of a normal product is consumed, the utility derived from consuming an additional unit of that product becomes less and less. This is called the law of diminishing marginal utility. A consumer maximizes satisfaction (attains equilibrium in consumption) when the price she is willing to pay for a product is equal to her marginal utility.

A producer will try to maximize profits by producing and selling the level of output where total sales revenue exceeds total cost by the greatest amount. At this point the marginal revenue earned is equal to the marginal cost incurred in the production of the product. In a competitive market to which we are referring, an individual producer is a price taker since she sells any given level of output at a price determined by the market. It follows that the price of a product is the same as the marginal revenue (the revenue derived from selling an extra unit of a product). A producer in a competitive market will, therefore, maximize profits when price is equal to marginal cost. If the price in the market goes up, the producer will sell more and the level of output she sells will be determined by the equality of marginal cost and price. If the price goes down, the producer will sell less output and the level of output will again be determined by equating marginal cost and price. The producer will move along her marginal cost curve and in this case supply becomes a positive function of price. As price goes up quantity supplied goes up and as price falls quantity supplied falls

---

[2] The utility concept will be developed fully in chapter three.

9

In the above discussion we have invoked what is known in economics as the equal marginal principle. Since the principle is widely used in economics, let us digress a little and try to understand what it is. In economics, maximizing or minimizing decisions are based on incremental or marginal reasoning. If a business firm's goal is to get the highest profit possible, we say that the firm is trying to maximize profits. Marginal reasoning in this case will be utilized if a firm looked at the sales revenue brought in by each successive product sold and weighed this against the cost of each successive product produced. The revenue associated with the sale of an extra unit of a product is called marginal revenue and the cost associated with the production of an extra unit of a product is called marginal cost. The equal marginal principle is involved when a balance between marginal values is used as an indicator of optimal (best) results. In our example, the best result is to have the highest profit possible and this is achieved when marginal cost is equal to marginal revenue[3].

Let us go back to our discussion of the competitive equilibrium market model. In chapter one, we defined the market system as a system where price allocates resources through the forces of supply and demand. What is demand and what is supply?

DEMAND:

Demand (for a product or service) is the amount consumers are **able** and **willing** to buy **at a given price** for a **period of time**. You will notice that, as in many expressions in economics, the definition of the word demand may differ from its ordinary English usage. You may understand demand to mean desire, need or want but the word is used differently in economics. Go back to the definition of demand. The buyers must be willing to buy a product, which means there is a need for the product but that is not enough. Desire must be accompanied by the ability to buy. You want the product and you have the ability to buy it but how much will you actually buy at given prices? This information should be very useful to a seller. When economists talk about demand they are interested in a pattern or tendency that can be observed or expected. Let us say you go to the grocery store at 12:00 pm and ask the manager to tell you the demand for milk during the last hour. The manager says that seven gallons have been bought. This information is not particularly useful because you will be left wondering what amount will be bought in the next hour or next day or the whole of next week or next month and so on. For the information on demand to be useful, you must observe sales data relative to prices for a long period of time. On the basis of this pattern or tendency you can predict, with a high degree of certainty, what the sales will be as long as other factors remain fixed.

THE LAW OF DEMAND:

Other things being equal (other factors remaining constant), the quantity demanded for a product is a negative (indirect) function of its price. As price goes down quantity demanded goes up and vice versa.

---

[3] Extensive applications of marginal reasoning and the equal marginal principle can be found in chapters 4, 6, 7, and 8.

As P↑   Q_d ↓
As P↓   Q_d ↑

This quantity/price relationship (the law of demand) can be depicted by a demand schedule, a demand curve, or a demand equation.

The hypothetical demand schedule below shows the quantity/price relationships for product X. We can see that as price goes up quantity demanded goes down and vice versa. This inverse relationship between price and quantity demanded is known as the law of demand.

DEMAND SCHEDULE	
PRICE (P)	QUANTITY DEMANDED (Q_d)
14	8
12	14
10	20
8	26
6	32
4	38
2	44

The quantity/price relationship in the above table can also be shown by the following demand curve. You will notice that the demand curve is downward sloping (has a negative slope) because of the inverse relationship between quantity demanded and price.

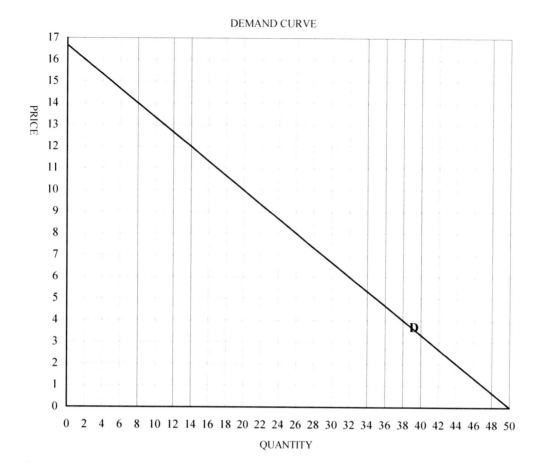

DEMAND CURVE

SUPPLY:

Supply (of a product or service) is the amount sellers are **able** and **willing** to sell **at a given price** for a **period of time.** Like in the case of demand, we are interested in some established pattern or tendency for the definition to be useful.

THE LAW OF SUPPLY:

Other things being equal, (other factors remaining constant) the quantity supplied of a product is a positive (direct) function of its price. As price goes up quantity supplied goes up and vice versa.

As P↑ Q_s ↑
As P↓ Q_s ↓

A person's willingness to supply a product in this case depends on how much money she makes on the product. She will always supply one more unit of a product as long as the price she gets for that unit is greater than what it costs to supply that unit. If price goes up relative to cost she will supply more because she will make more money. If price falls she will supply less. This tendency of reacting to price changes to supply less or more assumes a competitive market and the equal-marginal principle. It will become clear after studying microeconomics. For now let us assume that this direct relationship between price and quantity supplied exists and see how it may affect the market price for a product. Similarly, the quantity/price relationship (the law of supply) can be depicted by a supply schedule, a supply curve, or a supply equation.

The hypothetical supply schedule below shows the quantity/price relationships for product X. The supply schedule shows the desires of the producers to sell the product at various prices. In this case as price goes up quantity supplied goes up and as price falls, quantity supplied falls also. We called this direct relationship between quantity supplied and price the law of supply.

SUPPLY SCHEDULE	
PRICE (P)	QUANTITY SUPPLIED (Q_s)
14	38
12	34
10	30
8	26
6	22
4	18
2	14

The quantity/price relationship in the above table can also be shown by the following supply curve. You will notice that the supply curve is upward sloping (has a positive slope) because of the direct relationship between quantity supplied and price.

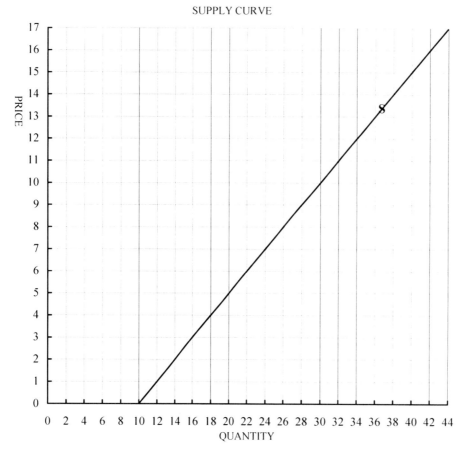

SUPPLY CURVE

Demand and supply schedules and demand and supply curves come from demand and supply equations that are estimated through a statistical method called regression analysis. In our example the demand equation is: $Q_d = 50\text{-}3P$ and the supply equation is: $Q_s = 10 + 2P$. From these equations you can determine every conceivable amount that will be demanded or supplied at any given price. The estimation of supply and demand functions and other economic functions is studied in an advanced course called econometrics. In most cases, as in this case, the functions used are hypothetical functions made up to explain a point.

THE INTERACTION OF CONSUMERS AND SUPPLIERS IN THE MARKET:

When consumers and producers interact in the market place, they are both guided by diametrically opposed motives. The buyers would like to have the lowest price possible for the product the sellers are selling and the sellers would like to have the highest price possible for their product. The market system will ensure that a satisfactory market price is established. The market price is also called the equilibrium price or the market-clearing price. This can be seen by superimposing the supply schedule on the demand schedule or the supply curve on the demand curve shown below.

PRICE	QUANTITY DEMANDED	QUANTITY SUPPLIED	
14	8	38	Qs>Qd by 30 = surplus
12	14	34	Qs>Qd by 20 = surplus
10	20	30	Qs>Qd by 10 = surplus
8	**26**	**26**	**Qs = Qd = 26** **Supply = Demand**
6	32	22	Qd>Qs by 10 = shortage
4	38	18	Qd>Qs by 20 = shortage
2	44	14	Qd>Qs by 30 = shortage

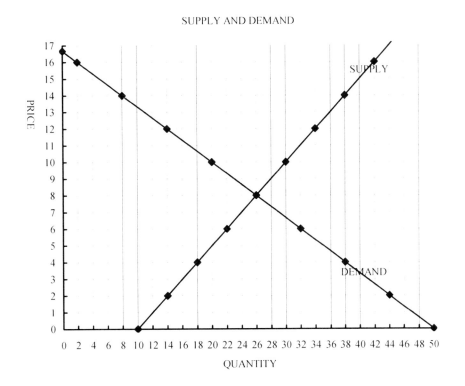

SUPPLY AND DEMAND

The price of $8 is the equilibrium price and the quantity of 26 is the equilibrium quantity. At the price of $8 we have an output that would satisfy consumer demand and at the same time satisfy the producers' desire for profit.

At the equilibrium price, all possible gains from trade by consumers and producers would be realized and any other price will leave either the producers or the consumers dissatisfied. Suppose, owing to wrong market signals, a price is established at $10. The price of $10 will be above the market-clearing price of $8 and it will lead to a surplus of 10 units in the market since quantity demanded will be 20 units and quantity supplied will be

30 units. Faced with rising inventories, which may be costly, producers will bid down prices until the equilibrium price is restored at $8. If, on the other hand, price is established below equilibrium say at $6 because of wrong market signals, there will be a shortage of 10 units in the market since quantity demanded will be 32 units and quantity supplied will be 22 units. In this case consumers will bid up prices through competition until equilibrium is restored at $8. According to the competitive equilibrium model, market forces will make corrections to temporary market imperfections and restore equilibrium without government involvement.

In a competitive market therefore, there will be an average price for a product that we call the equilibrium price. From time to time the price will be above or below the equilibrium price but the market model predicts that price will eventually tend towards the equilibrium price. The model also predicts that when supply and demand conditions change a new equilibrium price will be established.

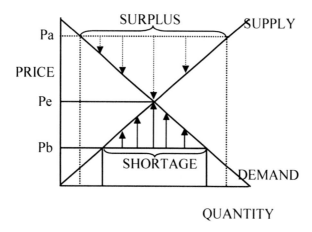

The diagram above shows how a competitive market works. If the market price is set above the equilibrium price by wrong market signals, there will be a surplus in the market. This will cause a downward pressure on price until equilibrium is restored at Pe. If the price is set below equilibrium by wrong market signals, there will be a shortage and this will cause an upward pressure on price until equilibrium is restored at Pe.

Why is the equilibrium price so important? It is important because for the price system to determine the composition of output and allocate resources efficiently, prices of different products must be determined through the forces of supply and demand in the manner we have described. The market mechanism must ensure that an ideal quantity of output is produced and a 'fair' price is charged. From society's perspective an output would be considered ideal if its price is equal to the opportunity cost of producing that output[4] . In

---

4 This relationship between marginal utility and marginal cost will be explained later in chapters
    three and six when we discuss utility and competition respectively.

other words an ideal output is produced when the consumer's marginal valuation of the product (i.e. marginal utility) is equal to the opportunity cost (i.e. marginal resource cost) of producing that product.

Marginal utility is measured by the price a consumer is willing to pay for a particular product. If, for example, the marginal cost of producing a pen is 50 cents and the price charged for that pen is also 50 cents, the pen in this case is being produced efficiently. The equality between marginal cost and price (P = MC) is an important necessary condition for achieving allocative efficiency or economic efficiency. From the above discussion we can see that allocative efficiency implies an ideal output and a 'fair' price, and it is achieved when the marginal valuation by consumers is equal to marginal cost. Another way of saying this is that the value of the product (price) reflects the true cost of producing the product (marginal cost). If the price charged is greater than marginal cost, as is the case with a monopoly, you will have under allocation of society's resources and if the price charged is less than marginal cost, as is the case with negative externalities, you will have over allocation of society's resources. Negative externalities occur when in the process of production or consumption, one party imposes a cost (harm) to another party and these costs are not reflected in market prices. A factory that pollutes a lake imposes a negative externality on the people who depend on the lake for their livelihood. The lake may be so contaminated that it kills all the marine life so that people cannot fish and water becomes a hazard to the people's health. In a case like this, the price charged does not reflect the actual costs involved. Price is less than marginal social cost[5].

APPLICATION OF THE COMPETITIVE EQUILIBRIUM MODEL:
PRICE CEILINGS AND PRICE FLOORS

Sometimes the government interferes with the operation of the market by imposing price ceilings and price floors. A price floor is a legal **minimum** price set **above** the equilibrium price, below which you cannot go. A price ceiling is a legal **maximum** price set **below** the equilibrium price, **above** which you cannot go. Examples of price floors are minimum wage and price supports given to farmers.

In the case of the minimum wage, the government looks at the wage rate set by the market and concludes that it is too low relative to the cost of living. In other words the government thinks that one cannot make a decent living on the wage rate determined by market forces and therefore requires employers to pay a wage that is higher than what the market would set. If we assume that there is a market for labor where labor as a factor is sold competitively, the wage rate acts as a surrogate price for labor.

Let us assume that the market determined wage rate (price for labor) for unskilled labor is $4.00 an hour. The government considers that wage rate to be too low and requires employers to pay $6.00 an hour. The graph below shows the theoretical consequences of this policy. The number of workers demanded by business declines from 7000 workers to 5000 workers and the number of workers willing to supply their labor at $6.00 an hour increases from 7000 to 9000. This causes a surplus of 4000 (9000-5000) in the labor

---

5 See chapters 3, 6, 7, and 10 for a detailed discussion of allocation efficiency, under allocation of resources, and over allocation of resources.

market. Those who believe in the free market oppose the idea of a minimum wage. They contend that the minimum wage causes unemployment and increases business costs. Other people would argue that it is not clear cut as the consequences would depend on the nature of the economy, the elasticity of supply and demand for labor, and the magnitude of the minimum wage rate.

A PRICE FLOOR ON THE LABOR MARKET

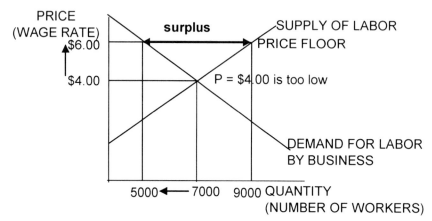

As for price supports, the government looks at the price set by the market for a product like milk and thinks the price is too low relative to the farmers' costs of production. To help the farmers, the government would set a price above the market price (equilibrium price). Again let us use the competitive equilibrium market model to discuss the theoretical consequences of a price support on the milk market. Left to its own devices the market would set the price of $1.50 per gallon, but the government wants the milk producers to get at least $2.50 per gallon. This is a little tricky though because the government cannot maintain the set price by decree as in the case of minimum wage. According to the laws of supply and demand, a higher price leads to less quantity demanded and more quantity supplied. Quantity demanded falls from 20,000 to 10,000 and quantity supplied increases from 20,000 to 30,000 thereby creating a surplus in the market. The surplus in this case would be 20,000 gallons (30,000 – 10,000).

To maintain the price of $2.50 the government may either buy the surplus or pay the farmers to produce less.

A PRICE FLOOR ON THE MILK MARKET

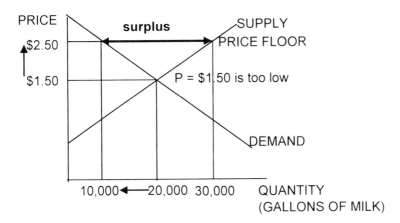

A price floor is a legal __minimum__ price set __above__ the equilibrium price, __below__ which you cannot go. Ex. minimum wage, price supports to farmers

A price ceiling is a legal **maximum** price set **below** the equilibrium price, **above** which you cannot go. In this case the government looks at price set by the market and thinks it is too high for the consumers. In some countries, governments set price ceilings (price controls) on some basic commodities like sugar and bread. In the 1970s the U.S. government imposed a price ceiling on the market for gasoline. Again the laws of supply and demand will lead to a shortage in the market as quantity demanded increases and quantity supplied decreases at a lower price.

Once again we use the competitive equilibrium market model to show the consequences of a price ceiling. Let us say some government considers bread a staple food product that should be available to everybody at a cheaper cost than the market would establish. In the example below, the market establishes the price of $2.00 but the government considers that price to be too high and therefore sets the price of $1.00 per loaf. Again according to the laws of supply and demand, a lower price leads to more quantity demanded and less quantity supplied. Quantity demanded rises from 3,000 to 4,000 and quantity supplied decreases from 3,000 to 2,000 thus creating a shortage of 2,000 loaves of bread (4,000 – 2,000

Note that the main consequence of price ceilings and floors is that they lead to a reduction in the quantity of goods traded in the market.

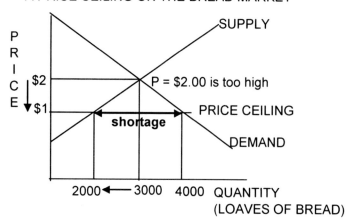

A PRICE CEILING ON THE BREAD MARKET

*A price ceiling is a legal **maximum** price set **below** the equilibrium price, **above** which you cannot go. Ex. rent control, price controls on gasoline in the 70s*

NON-PRICE DETERMINANTS OF DEMAND (OTHER FACTORS THAT AFFECT DEMAND)

The law of demand states that, other things being equal (other factors remaining constant), the quantity demanded of a product is an inverse (negative) function of its price. This means that there are other factors, other than price, that affect demand. These factors are called non-price determinants of demand and are assumed to remain fixed in any given demand function. The main non-price determinants of demand are consumer incomes, prices of related products (for example the prices of substitutes and complements), population (market size), consumer tastes and preferences, and government taxes and subsidies. Complements are products that are in joint demand. A car and gasoline, tea and sugar, bread and butter, etc. would be good examples of complements. Two products are considered substitutes if consumers are indifferent between the two. The examples of substitute goods are Pepsi and Coke, butter and margarine, and the different brands of soap and detergents.

When one of these non-price determinants of demand changes, a new demand pattern is established and the quantity price combinations change.

If consumer incomes were to increase, for example, there would be an **increase in demand**. This would mean that at every price now more would be bought than before. The demand curve will shift to the right (outward). On the graph below, the demand curve shifts to the right owing to income increase. At the price of eight dollars thirty units will be demanded instead of twenty-six that were demanded before the income increase. At the price of ten, twenty-four units will be demanded instead of twenty and so on. Similarly, an increase in the price of butter may lead to an increase in demand for margarine (a substitute). A decrease in price will have the opposite effects. A decrease in the price of tea may lead to an increase in the demand for sugar (a complement). A decrease in price will have the opposite effects.

AN INCREASE IN DEMAND

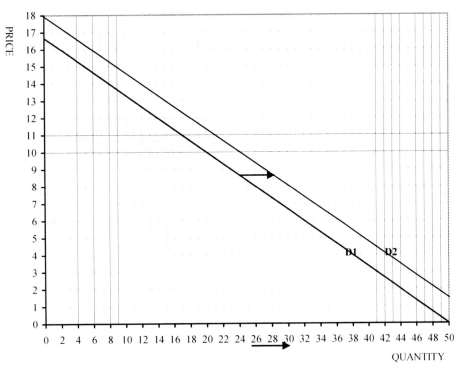

A DECREASE IN DEMAND

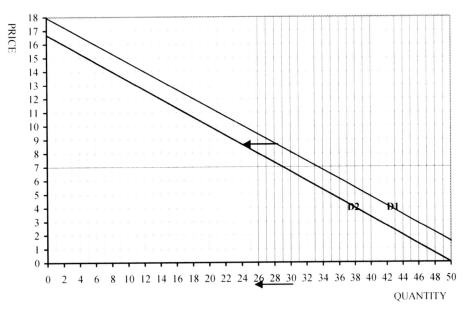

21

FACTORS THAT AFFECT DEMAND

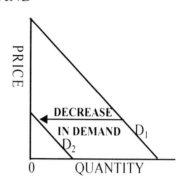

Demand will increase when
1) Income increases.
2) The price of a substitute increases.
3) The price of a complement decreases
4) Population (number of buyers) increases.
5) Income or price expectations increase.
6) There is a positive change in tastes or preferences.
7) The government reduces taxes or increases subsidies

Demand will decrease when
1) Income decreases.
2) The price of a substitute decreases.
3) The price of a complement increases.
4) Population (number of buyers) decreases.
5) Income or price expectations decrease.
6) There is a negative change in tastes or preferences.
7) The government increases taxes or reduces subsidies

THE DIFFERENCE BETWEEN A CHANGE IN DEMAND AND A CHANGE IN THE QUANTITY DEMANDED

A change in demand (increase or decrease) is a change in the entire pattern of demand caused by other factors other than price as shown in the graphs above. A shift of the whole demand curve (demand function) results when there is a change in demand. A change in the quantity demanded is caused by the price change of the product (i.e. by the law of demand). A change in the quantity demanded is depicted by a movement along the demand curve.

AN INCREASE IN DEMAND

An increase in demand, as a result of say an increase in consumer incomes, is depicted by an outward shift in the demand curve as shown in the following diagram we showed previously. On D1, quantity demanded is 20 when the price is $10.00. As price falls from $10.00 to $4.00, quantity demanded increases from 20 to 38. There has been a change in the **quantity demanded** as a result of a price change.

AN INCREASE IN DEMAND

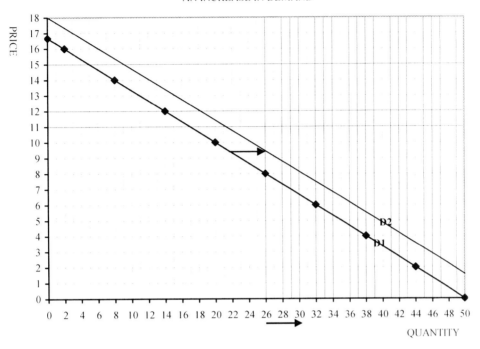

A DECREASE IN DEMAND

If incomes were to fall, the demand curve would shift to the left (inward) and less would be demanded at every price as you can see from the following diagram. Before the decrease in demand from D1 to D2, thirty units will be demanded at the price of eight dollars per unit. When demand decreases from D1 to D2, say as a result of a decrease in incomes, the quantity demanded at the price of eight will be twenty six units. At the price of ten, the quantity demanded will be twenty units instead of twenty-four units.

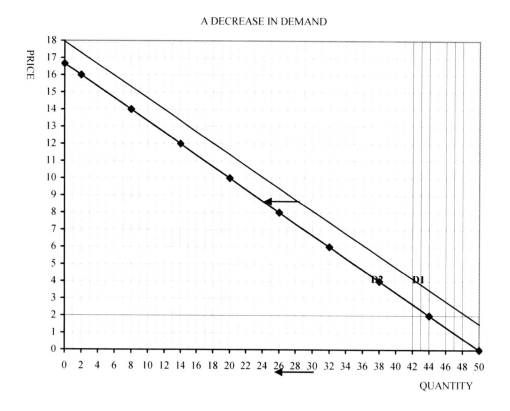

A DECREASE IN DEMAND

NON-PRICE DETERMINANTS OF SUPPLY (OTHER FACTORS THAT AFFECT SUPPLY)

The law of supply states that, other things being equal (other factors remaining constant), the quantity supplied of a product is a direct (positive) function of price. This means that in the case of supply there are also are other factors other than price that affect supply. These factors are called non-price determinants of supply. The non-price determinants of supply are cost of resources, the quantity of resources, the quality of resources, the nature of technology, the number of business firms in the industry (market size), subsidies, and the nature of the tax structure and regulations. Again when one of these factors changes, you will have a new supply pattern.

AN INCREASE IN SUPPLY

If the cost of resources were to decrease, for example, supply would increase and more would be supplied than before at every price. This means that the supply curve will shift to the right (outward) as can be seen from the graph below. At the price of eight dollars thirty two units will be supplied instead of twenty-six that were supplied before the decrease in resource cost. The business is able to supply more and remain profitable because of the lower costs of production.

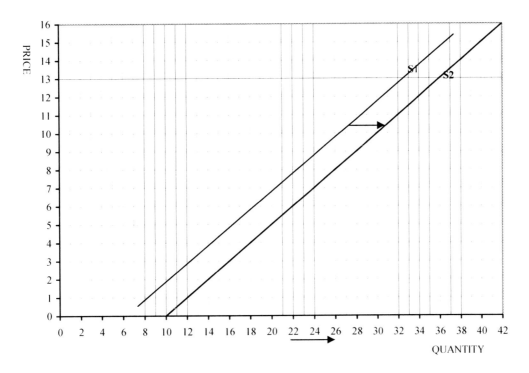

AN INCREASE IN SUPPLY

25

A DECREASE IN SUPPLY

 If, on the other hand, the cost of resources were to rise, less output will be supplied at every price and the supply curve would shift to the left (inward).

A DECREASE IN SUPPLY

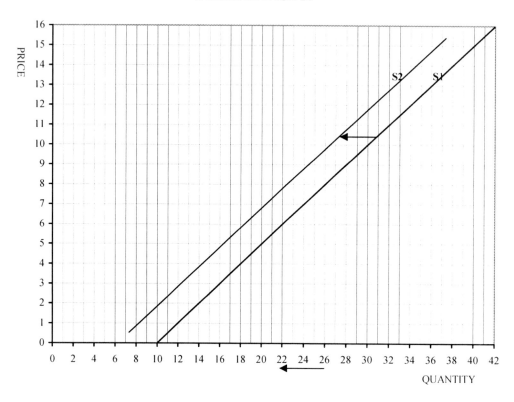

FACTORS THAT AFFECT SUPPLY

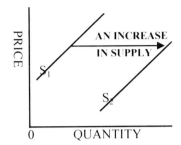

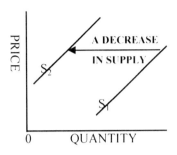

Supply will increase when
1) Technology improves.
2) The cost of resources falls.
3) The number of sellers increases.
4) The government reduces taxes or increases subsidies.
5) The government reduces business regulations.
6) Prices of related products (substitutes in production) increase.

Supply will decrease when
1) Technology declines.
2) The cost of resources rises.
3) The number of sellers decreases.
4) The government increases taxes or reduces subsidies.
5) The government increases business regulations.
6) Prices of related products (substitutes in production) increase.

THE DIFFERENCE BETWEEN A CHANGE IN SUPPLY AND A CHANGE IN THE QUANTITY SUPPLIED

A change in supply (increase or decrease) is a change in the entire pattern of supply caused by other factors other than price. A shift of the whole supply curve results when there is a change in supply. The following diagram shows an increase in supply (the supply curve shifts from S1 to S2). A change in the quantity supplied is caused by the price change of the product (i.e. by the law of supply). This leads to a movement along the supply curve. On S2, for example, quantity supplied increases from 22 to 34 units as price increases from $6.00 to $12.00.

AN INCREASE IN SUPPLY

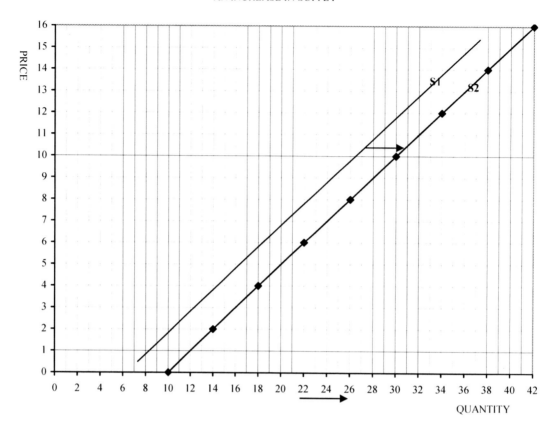

ANOTHER LOOK AT THE DIFFERENCE BETWEEN A CHANGE IN DEMAND VERSUS A CHANGE IN THE QUANTITY DEMANDED AND A CHANGE IN SUPPLY VERSUS A CHANGE IN THE QUANTITY SUPPLIED

A CHANGE IN DEMAND VERSUS A CHANGE IN THE QUANTITY DEMANDED

A change in demand (increase or decrease) means a shift in the entire demand curve caused by changes in other factors other than price. A change in the quantity demanded means a movement along the demand curve caused by a change in price.

A CHANGE IN DEMAND

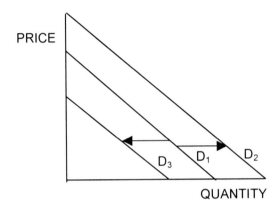

A CHANGE IN THE QUANTITY DEMANDED

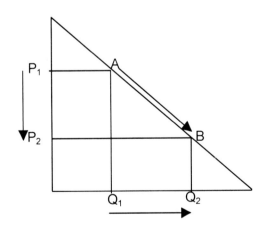

29

A CHANGE IN SUPPLY VERSUS A CHANGE IN THE QUANTITY SUPPLIED
A change in supply (increase or decrease) means a shift in the entire supply curve caused by changes in other factors other than price.

A CHANGE IN SUPPLY

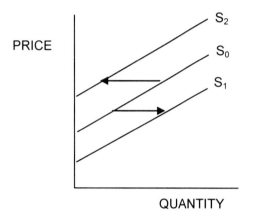

A change in the quantity supplied means a movement along the supply curve caused by the change in price. A movement from A to B, for example, indicates a change in the quantity supplied.

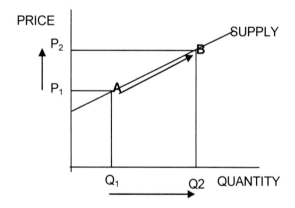

THE EFFECTS OF THE CHANGES IN THE FORCES OF SUPPLY AND DEMAND
The supply and demand curves presented above are constructed based on certain conditions existing at a particular period of time. Over time these conditions change and therefore new demand and supply curves will have to be drawn. Overtime, for example,

people may change their preferences for or against a product because of advertising or the introduction of new similar products. Over time, supply may be affected by changes in technology, changes in government regulations, or changes in the cost of resources. In this case you will have a new set of market conditions.

When market conditions change, the competitive equilibrium market model predicts that the market price (equilibrium price) and the quantity of the product traded in the market will be affected. If, for example, consumer incomes were to increase (the demand curve shifts outward) and the conditions of supply were to remain the same (the supply curve does not shift) we predict that the market price will go up and the quantity exchanged in the market will also go up.

Initially an increase in demand without a change in supply causes a shortage, which puts an upward pressure on price. Sellers will supply more until a new equilibrium is established at a higher price and higher output. The graph below shows that when demand increases from D_1 to D_2 price rises from \$8 to \$10 and quantity rises from 26 units to 30 units.

THE EFFECTS OF AN INCREASE IN DEMAND

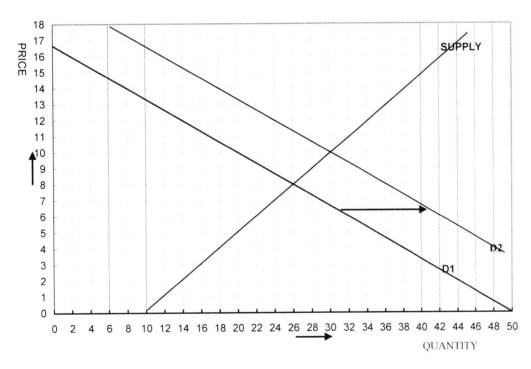

We also saw that if consumer incomes were to decrease (the demand curve shifts inward) and the conditions of supply were to remain the same, (the supply curve does not shift) the market price will go down and the quantity exchanged in the market will also go down. You can see these effects if you move from D_1 to D_2 in the graph below. Price falls from \$8 to \$6 and quantity exchanged falls from 26 units to 22 units.

31

THE EFFECTS OF A DECREASE IN DEMAND

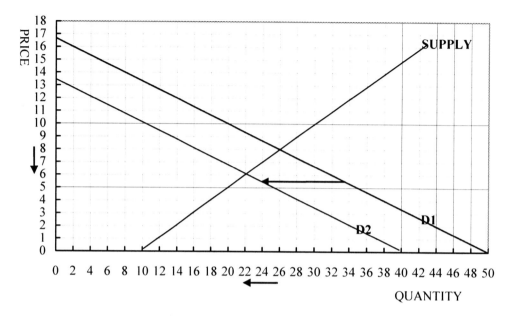

If supply was to increase because of the reduction in the costs of resources (the supply curve shifts outward) and if demand conditions were to remain the same (the demand curve does not shift), we predict that the market price will fall and the quantity exchanged in the market will rise. An increase in supply without an increase in demand causes a surplus which puts a downward pressure on price. Consumers will buy more at a lower price and a new equilibrium will be established at a lower price and higher output. The graph below shows that when supply increases from S_1 to S_2 price falls from \$8 to \$6 and quantity rises from 26 units to 32 units.

THE EFFECTS OF AN INCREASE IN SUPPLY

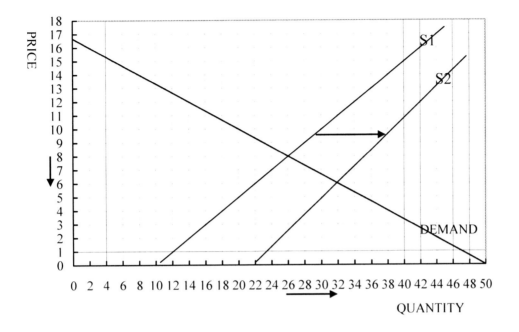

If the costs of production were to increase (the supply curve shifts inward) and demand conditions were to remain the same, (the demand curve does not shift) we predict that the market price will go up and the quantity exchanged in the market will go down. You can see these outcomes if you move from S_1 to S_2 on the graph below. Price rises from $8 to $10 and quantity falls from 26 units to 20 units.

THE EFFECTS OF A DECREASE IN SUPPLY

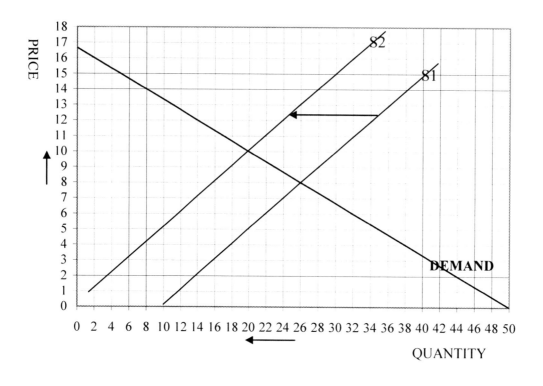

A SUMMARY OF THE EFFECTS OF DEMAND AND SUPPLY CHANGES

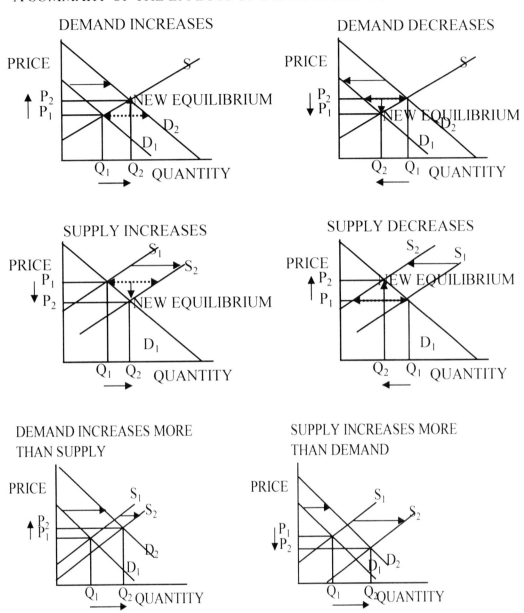

Show with graphs what happens to equilibrium price and quantity when: a) demand decreases more than supply, b) supply decreases more than demand, and c) both supply and demand increase in the same proportion.

TIME AND ADJUSTMENT OF SUPPLY AND DEMAND

So far we have assumed that there are instantaneous changes in price and quantity when forces of supply and demand change but in reality this may not be the case. It takes time for consumers to realize that prices have changed unless price changes are drastic.

It may also take time to switch to other products because of lack of information on the new products. Adjusting to a new equilibrium price may therefore take time. In the long run it is easier to adjust as more information becomes available. It also takes time to adjust to a new equilibrium price when supply forces change. Producers may not respond quickly because it takes time and expense to increase capacity, acquire more inputs, get rid of old fixed inputs, and change contractual obligations.

Economic terms to remember:

Demand	A change in supply
Supply	A change in the quantity supplied
The law of demand	A price floor
The law of supply	A price ceiling
Equilibrium price	
A change in demand	
A change in the quantity demanded	

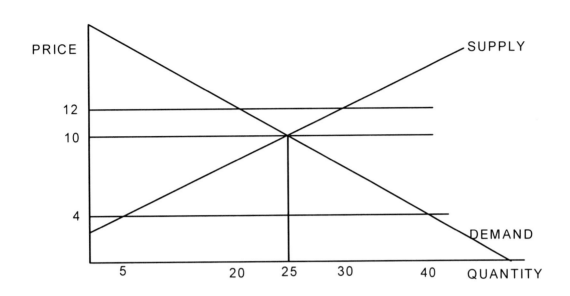

Use the <u>diagram above</u> (not drawn to scale) depicting the market conditions for good X to answer the following questions:

a) What is the equilibrium price?...............................

b) What amount of output (quantity) is **bought** at that price?.....

c) What amount of output is **sold** at the equilibrium price?.......

d) What is the **total** consumer **expenditure** at the equilibrium price?...........

e) How much sales revenue (**Total Revenue**) do the producers get at the equilibrium price?........

f) Of the three prices given what price would you consider a price ceiling?.............

g) Of the three prices given what price would you consider a price floor?..............

h) Of the three prices given what price leads to a surplus (excess supply)?...........

i) What is the amount of the surplus?........................

j) How much output should the government buy to make the price floor effective?.........

k) Of the three prices given what price leads to a shortage (excess demand)?.........

l) What is the amount of the shortage?........................

m) What would happen to price, quantity demanded and quantity supplied if the price ceiling was removed?(i.e. rise, fall or same)

   (i) price.......................…………………………………...By how much?...........

   (ii) quantity demanded…………..…………...…..By how much?...........

   (iii) quantity supplied……………………………......By how much?...........

n) What would happen to price, quantity demanded and quantity supplied if the price floor was removed? (i.e. rise, fall or same)

   (i) price…..……………….…..............By how much?...........

   (ii) quantity demanded….......……....By how much?...........

   (iii) quantity supplied……….…..........By how much?...........

n) What would happen to equilibrium price, quantity traded of good X if the price of good Y, which is a close substitute, was to fall? (ASSUMING OTHER MARKET CONDITIONS DO NOT CHANGE, MODIFY THE DIAGRAM TO SHOW THE ABOVE EFFECT)

(i) Price... (ii) Quantity traded................................

2) Use a **supply and demand** diagram (**one supply and demand graph**) to explain why good weather that leads to a good wheat harvest may actually be bad for wheat farmers. Assume wheat is sold in a competitive market.

3). With the help of a graph (supply and demand diagram) explain why some politicians and economists oppose government **price ceilings** on products like gasoline.

4) Use the competitive equilibrium market model to predict the outcome, **in the short run,** of the change described in A, B, & C, and answer the associated questions using the following letters: R = rises, F = falls, N = no change,

(Don't forget the differences between a change in demand and a change in the quantity demanded and a change in supply and a change in the quantity supplied). A graph is always helpful.

A) A product's **cost of production** falls. The variables below change as follows

    Supply

    Demand

    Price

    Quantity traded (equilibrium quantity)

B) More sellers are drawn into the market for good Z by the prospect of making high profits. The variables below change as follows:

    Supply:

    Demand

    Price

    Quantity traded (equilibrium quantity)

C) More buyers are drawn into the market for good K because of advertising. The variables below change as follows

    Supply

    Demand

    Price

    Quantity traded (equilibrium quantity)

CHAPTER 3: CONSUMER CHOICE (THE THEORY OF CONSUMER BEHAVIOR)

Economists use utility theory to describe consumer behavior. Utility is the satisfaction a consumer gets from the consumption of a product. This satisfaction may, in some cases, be difficult to describe. We can describe the satisfaction we get from eating food or driving a car but how does one describe the satisfaction one gets from smoking a cigarette to a non-smoker?

Let assume that each individual knows and can describe the utility derived from consuming a product. The next problem to contend with is how to measure this satisfaction. How do you measure satisfaction derived from wearing a hat? drinking beer? watching a ball game? etc. The solution has been to measure utility in terms of the money price one is willing to pay for a product or service. I terms of measurement, it is useful to distinguish between total utility and marginal utility. Total utility is the maximum amount of money one is willing to pay for a product. Marginal utility is the amount of money one is willing to pay for an extra unit of a product. Economists, as you will see shortly, are interested in the concept of marginal utility.

A consumer reveals her preferences for the product by the price she is willing to pay for that product. If you are willing to pay twenty dollars for your hat, twenty dollars would be a measure of the satisfaction you get from that particular hat. Your friend who does not like hats may not be willing to get your hat even for free. The hat in that case has no value to her since she is not willing to have it even for free.

THE LAW OF DIMINISHING MARGINAL UTILITY:

It is a general observation that as more of a normal product[6] is consumed, the utility derived from consuming an additional unit of that product (marginal utility) becomes less and less. This is called the law of diminishing marginal utility. Let us say you go home one evening after a day's hard work and you feel thirsty. You immediately rush to your refrigerator and get a glass of water to quench your thirst. After the first glass you feel you want another one and you go ahead and take the second glass. Do you go for the third one? forth? fifth? Chances are you will stop at two or one and half. The second glass will give you less satisfaction (utility) than the first one and the third one will give you less satisfaction than the second one and so on. At some point, actually taking more and more may be harmful. In that case marginal utility will be negative.

On the basis of the law of diminishing marginal utility one will be inclined to pay less and less for the product because the value (utility) becomes less and less. You are not likely to pay the same amount for the forth hat as the first hat, unless you are a hat collector.

The table below and the accompanying graph show a total utility function for a normal good (meat). The function is increasing at a decreasing rate. As the consumption of meat increases, the slope of the function (change in TU divided by the change in pounds bought) becomes less and less (i.e. the marginal utility falls for every unit bought) and the

---

[6] A normal product is a product whose demand increases as income increases and demand falls as income falls. The opposite of a normal good is an inferior good whose demand falls as income increases and demand increases as income falls.

function reaches a maximum at eight units. The slope at that point is zero, and beyond that it becomes negative.

POUNDS OF MEAT (LBS)	TOTAL UTILITY (TU)	MARGINAL UTILITY (MU)
0	0	0
1	3.75	3.75
2	7.00	3.25
3	9.75	2.75
4	12.00	2.25
5	13.75	1.75
6	15.00	1.25
7	15.75	0.75
8	16.00	0.25
9	15.75	-0.25
10	15.00	-0.75
11	13.75	-1.25
12	12.00	-1.75
13	9.75	-2.25

A UTILITY FUNCTION FOR A NORMAL GOOD

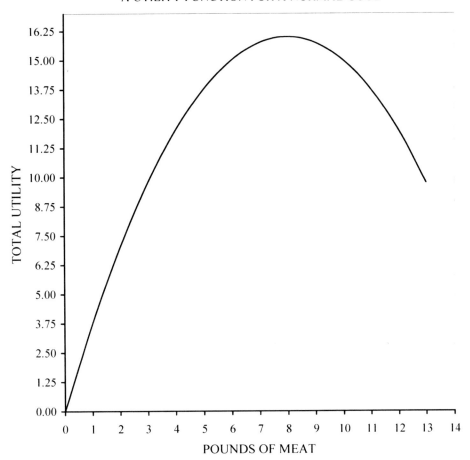

UTILITY FUNCTIONS
WITH DIFERENT BEHAVIORS

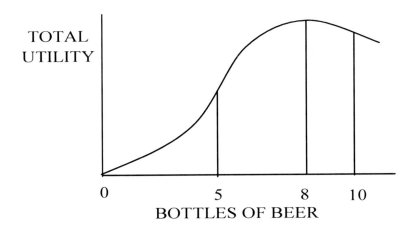

41

The above utility function increases at an increasing rate up to the fifth bottle. It then increases at a decreasing rate after fifth bottle and reaches a maximum at eight bottles. After the eighth bottle the marginal utility is negative. Every time I ask my students to give an example of a product that exhibits the above tendencies, they always say beer. Whether you agree with them or not, these students are suggesting that marginal utility increases, for example, with each extra bottle taken up to the fifth bottle. After the fifth bottle, marginal utility declines with each extra bottle taken and after the eighth bottle marginal utility becomes negative. I guess at the fifth bottle one starts getting uncomfortable. (Note: For some people marginal utility would start declining after the third bottle or even the second one but you get the idea). Beyond the eighth bottle the marginal utility becomes negative. May be somebody is getting sick at this point or falling off the chair or lying on the floor? Could the cliché that 'too much of anything is harmful' be true in this case?

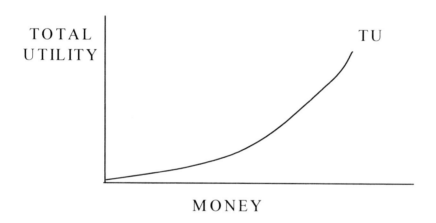

In the above utility function, marginal utility increases the more you have of an item. Some people, including myself, believe that the more money you have the greater satisfaction you get. Other things often mentioned that would demonstrate these tendencies are collectors' items like stamps and antiques.

CONSUMER EQUILIBRIUM (THE OPTIMAL PURCHASE RULE)
    A consumer maximizes satisfaction (attains equilibrium in consumption) when the price she is willing to pay for a product is equal to her marginal utility. If we consider price (P) as cost and marginal utility (MU) as benefit, a consumer will maximize her utility when cost (price) is equal to benefit (marginal utility).
    P = MU is the condition for utility maximization with one product. This condition for consumer equilibrium (utility maximization) is also called the optimal purchase rule. It can also be shown that the concept of benefit and cost as used here, can be used to establish equilibrium conditions with two products but that is beyond this book.

If price (cost) is **less** than marginal utility (benefit) the consumer should buy **more** until P (cost) = MU (benefit)

If price (cost) is **greater** than marginal utility (benefit) the consumer should buy **less** until P (cost) = MU (benefit)

Note: At equilibrium price must be equal to MU or it could be less (as long as they are close) than MU, but price should **never** be greater than MU.

Let us revisit the table depicting the utility function for meat.

LBS	MU
0	0
1	3.75
2	3.25
3	2.75
4	2.25
5	1.75
6	1.25
7	0.75
8	0.25
9	-0.25

Suppose the selling price for meat per pound was $3.50. According to the consumer maximization rule established above, the consumer should buy one pound of meet. Why not two pounds? The second pound will bring in less benefits relative to cost (MU=3.25) < (P=3.50). If the price was at 2.50 then the buyer should buy 3 pounds, at P = $1.50, buy 5 pounds and at P = $0.75, buy 7 pounds. Examine this relationship in the following table:

PRICE	QUANTITY
$3.50	1
$2.50	3
$1.50	5
$0.75	7

What does this relationship remind you of? The law of demand of course.

If a consumer is initially in equilibrium, price must be lowered to convince her to buy more. This is so because additional units of the product will result in lower marginal utility. If the price was to remain at the previous level, price (cost) will be greater than marginal utility (benefit) and the consumer will not be maximizing her utility. This is the logic used to explain why the demand curve for a consumer is downward sloping. You will recall that the demand curve is a geometrical representation of the law of demand, which states that, other things being equal, quantity demanded of a product, is an inverse function of its 'own' price. For the consumer, the relationship between consumer demand and price is indirect in that as price goes up quantity demanded goes down and as price goes down quantity demanded goes up. Consumers reveal their preferences about a product by the amount they are able and willing to buy at different prices. As explained below, we make a horizontal summation of individual demand curves to get a market demand curve.

You may have noticed that some demand curves are drawn like the one below with some quantity demanded at the price of zero. At the price of zero the amount demanded is seven. Why not more than seven? Why the limit of seven units when the product is being offered for free? Even at the price of zero people have a limit in terms of what they can have? You never see people who get 'free' goods like cheese with truckloads of cheese. Suppose some rich individual was giving out free cars and you were told to take as many as you wanted on the condition that you could not resell them or give them away. How many cars do you think you would grab? Even for a valuable product like a car, the law of diminishing marginal utility applies. Except for money of course!

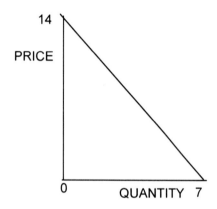

DERIVING THE MARKET DEMAND CURVE

The market demand curve is derived from the addition of the quantities that each individual person is willing to buy at each price. The market demand curve is the horizontal summation of the individual demand curves. For demonstration purposes let us use two individuals namely Joe and Jane to show how a market demand curve is derived. Joe is willing to buy 4 pounds of meat per week at $5 per pound and Jane is willing to buy 7 pounds of meat per week at $5 per pound. The total quantity demanded by both of them (market demand) at the price of $5 per pound is 11 pounds. At the price of $3 per pound Joe is willing to buy 6 pounds per week and Jane is willing to buy 9 pounds per week. The total quantity demanded by both of them (market demand) at the price of $3 per pound is 15 pounds. The same method can be used to derive a market demand curve for many more individuals. When we discussed utility theory in chapter 3, we concluded that price measures marginal utility. It follows then that when we add up individual demand curves, we are actually adding up marginal utilities (marginal benefits). The market demand curve is therefore a horizontal summation of the individuals' marginal benefits (MBs).

Demand = D = Price = ΣMBs.

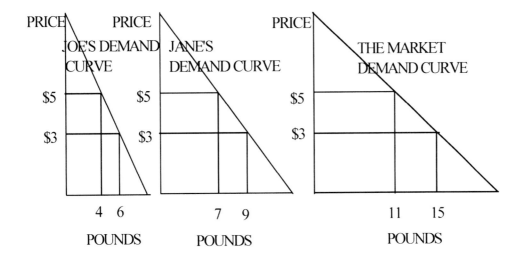

THE WATER DIAMOND PARADOX

We can use the marginal utility concept to explain the water diamond paradox. Water, which is essential to life, is cheaper relative to diamonds, which are not essential to life. In other words the relative exchange for diamonds is higher than that of water. If you went door to door trying to sell water (even bottled water), you would not get as much as you would get selling diamonds. This is a paradox because we would have expected water to cost relatively more than diamonds, which are not essential to life. It is said that water has a high value in use but a low value in exchange whereas diamonds have a low value in use but a high value in exchange. This paradox has a two-part explanation. One has to do with supply and another has to do with marginal utility. Diamonds are scarce and expensive to produce and therefore are supplied at a higher price. People have few diamonds on account of a high price and therefore its marginal utility is high. Water is plentiful and it is supplied at a lower price and therefore it has low marginal utility. According to the optimal purchase rule discussed earlier people are willing to pay a low price if the marginal utility derived from a product is low and a high price if the marginal utility derived from a product is high. The marginal utility of water determines its price and not its total utility. If you were stranded in desert without water, though, I bet you would be willing to exchange your diamonds for a bottle of water without hesitation. In that case water would have a higher value in exchange than the diamonds.

Economic concepts to remember:

Utility	total utility
Marginal utility	market demand
A normal good	an inferior good
Equilibrium in consumption	the optimal purchase rule
The law of diminishing marginal utility	

CHAPTER 4: DEMAND AND SUPPLY ELASTICITY

ELASTICITY OF DEMAND

To understand the concept of price elasticity of demand one must revisit the law of demand. The law of demand states that there is an inverse relationship between the quantity demanded of a product and its price. This merely tells us the direction of change in the amount demanded as price changes but it does not tell us the magnitude of this change. The elasticity concept measures the **responsiveness** or the **sensitivity** of the quantity demanded to price change. It helps us to determine the degree of responsiveness of quantity demanded to price change.

This is a useful tool that can be used in pricing and taxation policies. If we know the coefficient of price elasticity of demand we can tell whether total sales revenue will fall or rise if we were to change the price of our product. The government will be able to determine what products to tax and to estimate how much tax revenue it is likely to collect.

The coefficient of elasticity of demand is simply a number that measures the degree of responsiveness of demand to price change. It is similar in concept to the slope of a function but, unlike the slope, it is not affected by the problems of scale or the units of measurement used.

The coefficient of elasticity of demand (Ed) is calculated by dividing the percentage change in quantity to the percentage change in price.

$$Ed = \frac{\%\Delta \text{ in } Q}{\%\Delta \text{ in } P}$$

The ratio above is calculated in two ways, depending on whether the change in price is big or infinitely small. For a big change we use a mid-point formula (the range formula).This is also called arc-elasticity of demand.

For a very small change we use the point elasticity formula called point elasticity of demand.

ELASTICITY OF DEMAND

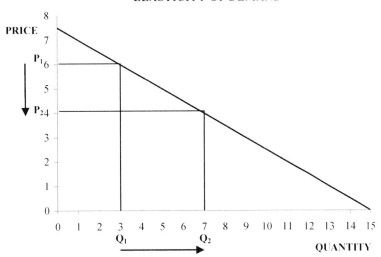

$$\text{Arc Ed} = \frac{\text{Change in quantity}}{(\text{Sum of quantities})/2} \div \frac{\text{Change in price}}{(\text{Sum of prices})/2}$$

The expression above can be rewritten as follows:

$$\text{Arc Ed} = \frac{Q_2 - Q_1}{(Q_2 + Q_1)/2} \div \frac{P_2 - P_1}{(P_2 + P_1)/2}$$

$$\text{Arc Ed} = \frac{\dfrac{Q_2 - Q_1}{(Q_2 + Q_1)/2}}{\dfrac{P_2 - P_1}{(P_2 + P_1)/2}}$$

The twos cancel out and the expression simplifies to the following:

$$\text{Arc Ed} = \frac{\dfrac{Q_2 - Q_1}{Q_2 + Q_1}}{\dfrac{P_2 - P_1}{P_2 + P_1}}$$

We can simplify it even further with the following results[7]:

$$\text{Arc Ed} = \frac{(Q_2 - Q_1)(P_2 + P_1)}{(P_2 - P_1)(Q_2 + Q_1)} = \frac{\Delta Q(P_2 + P_1)}{\Delta P(Q_2 + Q_1)},$$

$$\text{Arc Ed} = \frac{\Delta Q(P_2 + P_1)}{\Delta P(Q_2 + Q_1)}$$

---

[7] We use this complicated formula to determine percentage change in quantity over percentage change in Price ($Ed = \dfrac{\%\Delta \text{ in } Q}{\%\Delta \text{ in } P}$) because, with a big change, the percentage change when price falls is different from the percentage change when price rises. Also the percentage change when quantity falls is different from the percentage change when quantity rises. The percentage change from 6 to 4 is 33% whereas the percentage change from 4 to 6 is 50%. The percentage change from 7 to 3 is 57% while the percentage change from 3 to 7 is 133%. To deal with this problem we add prices and divide by two to get a mid-point and we do the same thing to the quantities. This is why the formula is also called the mid-point formula. See graph below:

ELASTICITY OF DEMAND

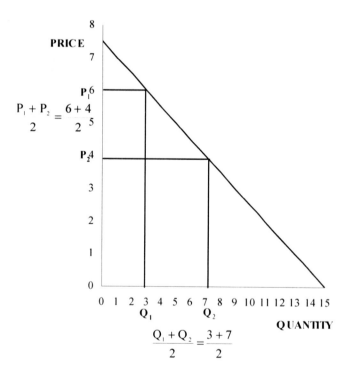

For interpretation purposes, we take the absolute value of the coefficient.

In this case we are interested in the magnitude of the number so we ignore the negative sign. Use the Arc Ed formula to confirm that the coefficient of elasticity demand in the price range of 6 to 4 on the previous graph (titled Elasticity of Demand) is -2.

A coefficient of two means that if price was increased by one percent, quantity demanded would decrease by two percent and a decrease in price of one percent would lead to a two-percentage increase in quantity demanded. Armed with this useful information, we can now predict what the change in quantity demanded will be for any percentage change in price. For example, given that the elasticity of demand is two, a 15% change in price will result in a 30% change in quantity demanded.

The absolute values of elasticity coefficients range from zero to infinity.

A coefficient of zero implies demand is perfectly inelastic. In other words demand is completely unresponsive to price change. An example of a product with this type of demand would be medicine.

If the coefficient is less than one, demand is relatively inelastic (inelastic). This means that a certain percentage change in price leads to a smaller percentage change in quantity demanded. Gasoline, food, cigarettes, electricity, and alcohol are good examples of the products with inelastic demand.

If the coefficient is greater than one, demand is considered to be relatively elastic (elastic). In this case a certain percentage change in price leads to a bigger percentage change in quantity demanded. All products with good substitutes will have elastic demand.

If the coefficient is infinity (indeterminate), demand is perfectly elastic. Products with perfect substitutes will have this type of demand[8]. The coefficient of one indicates that demand is unitary elastic.

The following graphs show the elasticities of different demand curves when evaluated at the same point.

---

[8] Perfectly elastic demand will be explained later when we discuss perfect competition in chapter 6

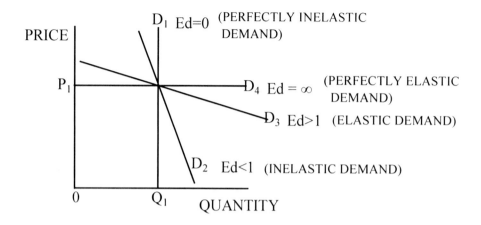

POINT ELASTICITY OF DEMAND

Point elasticity of demand is used to measure the responsiveness of quantity demanded to price change for an infinitesimal change in price.
It is the price elasticity at a specific point on the demand curve.

$$Ed = \frac{\%\Delta \text{ in } Q}{\%\Delta \text{ in } P}$$

$$Ed = \frac{\dfrac{\Delta Q}{Q}}{\dfrac{\Delta P}{P}} = \frac{\Delta Q \times P}{\Delta P \times Q} = \left(\frac{dQ}{dP}\right) \times \frac{P}{Q}$$

The reciprocal of the slope

a) Use the following demand function to compute the coefficients of elasticity of demand at point A (when price = $3) and point B (when price = $1).
b) Is demand relatively elastic or inelastic at point A? c) What about at point B?
c) What is the coefficient of elasticity of demand when price = $2?
Demand function: Q = 20 – 5P

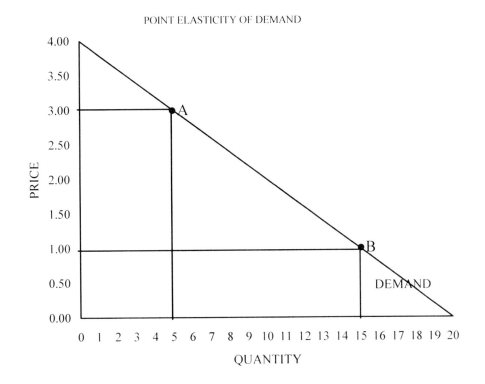

POINT ELASTICITY OF DEMAND

THE RELATIONSHIP BETWEEN PRICE, ELASTICITY OF DEMAND, AND TOTAL SALES REVENUE (TOTAL REVENUE)

When demand is inelastic (i.e. a % Δ Q is < a %Δ P), total revenue falls as price falls and total revenue rises as price rises. If demand is elastic (i.e. a % Δ in Q is > a % Δ in P), total revenue rises as price falls and it falls as price rises. If the coefficient is one (i.e. a % Δ in Q is = a Δ %) in P), total revenue will remain the same as price changes[9].

---

[9] See the discussion about the relationship between marginal revenue and total revenue in chapter seven.

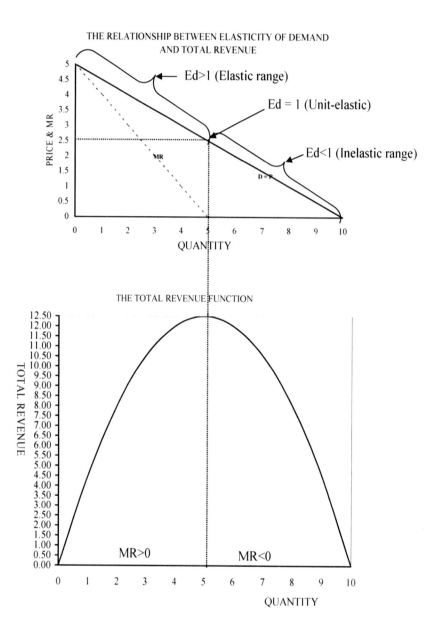

THE RELATIONSHIP BETWEEN ELASTICITY OF DEMAND
AND TOTAL REVENUE

THE TOTAL REVENUE FUNCTION

The above diagram shows how total revenue changes as price falls on a linear demand curve. In the elastic range of demand, a price decrease causes total revenue to increase. Total revenue reaches a maximum when elasticity is unitary.

In the inelastic range of demand, a price decrease causes total revenue to fall.

CROSS ELASTICITY OF DEMAND

The coefficient of cross elasticity of demand is used to measure sensitivity of demand across goods and across markets.

$$\text{Cross Ed}(E_{xy}) = \frac{\%\Delta Q_x}{\%\Delta P_y} = \frac{\%\Delta \text{ in the Q of Coke}}{\%\Delta \text{ in the P of Pepsi}}$$

In this case the signs must be maintained. If the coefficient is negative, it means the two products are complements and if it is positive it means the two products are substitutes. A coefficient of greater than one means that the two products are competitive in the same market.

Cross elasticity of demand is used for market definitions. It can be used, for example, to tell whether natural gas is competing with electricity. It is also used for pricing strategies both in-house (similar products within the company) and similar products outside the company.

It is also used for anti-trust cases. A coefficient that is larger than one indicates that the products are competitive in the same market (the bigger the coefficient the greater the competition). A coefficient of less than one means there is less competition.

ELASTICITY OF SUPPLY

Elasticity of supply measures the responsiveness of quantity supplied to price change. The interpretation of the size of the elasticity coefficient is the same as that of demand elasticity.

$$Es = \frac{\%\Delta Qs}{\%\Delta P}$$

If the coefficient is equal to zero, supply is perfectly inelastic. If the coefficient is less than one, supply is considered to be relatively inelastic (inelastic). If the coefficient is greater than one, supply is considered to be relatively elastic. In this case a certain percentage change in price leads to a bigger percentage change in quantity supplied. If the coefficient is infinite, (indeterminate) supply is perfectly elastic.

The following graphs show the elasticities of different supply curves when evaluated at the same point.

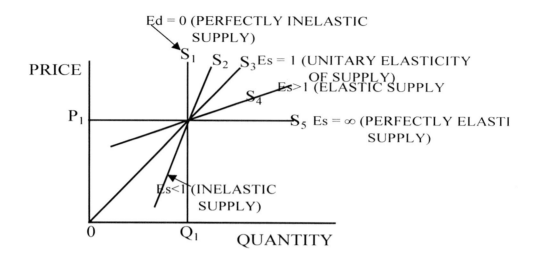

INCOME ELASTICITY OF DEMAND

The coefficient of income elasticity of demand is used to measure the sensitivity of demand to income change.

$$\text{Income Ed.}(E_i) = \frac{\%\Delta Q}{\%\Delta \text{Income}}$$

The signs must be maintained in this case also. If the coefficient is less than one it means the product is a necessity. If it is greater than one the product is considered a luxury. A positive coefficient implies a normal product and a negative coefficient implies an inferior product. A normal product is a product whose demand goes up as income increases and demand falls as income falls. An inferior product is a product whose demand falls as income increases and demand rises as income falls. Try to imagine an individual whose weekly budget can only allow the consumption of the cheapest inferior food product. If this individual gets richer, she will buy more of the superior product and less of the inferior product and if income falls she will buy less of the superior item and more of the inferior item because the inferior item is cheaper.

ELASTICITY AND THE INCIDENCE OF A TAX

UNIT TAX = $4

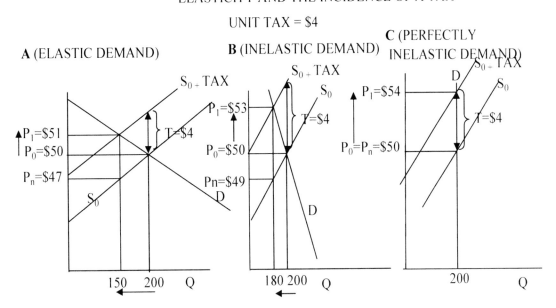

A (ELASTIC DEMAND)   **B (INELASTIC DEMAND)**   **C (PERFECTLY INELASTIC DEMAND)**

a) Demand elasticity and the tax incidence.

Tax incidence deals with the question of who ultimately bears the burden of a tax. In market A, S_0 and D are supply and demand curves for sneakers before a sales tax of $4 per pair is imposed. The price established by the market before the tax is $50.00 and 200 pairs are sold a week.

As a result of the tax the suppliers are forced to supply at a higher cost and this causes a vertical shift of the supply curve by the amount of the tax. Since demand does not change, a new equilibrium price is established at $51. Buyers are now paying a higher price ($51) that is higher than the original price of $50 because of the tax. This means that the consumers contribute $1 to tax payment.

The producers pay the rest of the tax ($3) and the net amount they receive per pair (producers' supply price) is reduced by the amount of the tax paid (i.e.$50 - $3 = $47).

The effects of the tax are summarized below:

In market model A, the tax paid by consumers is: $P_1 - P_0 = Tc = \$51 - \$50 = \$1$ per pair. Total taxes paid by buyers = 150 x $1 = $150.

The tax paid by producers is: $P_0 + T - P_1 = Tp = (\$50 + \$4) - \$51 = \$3$ per pair.

$Tp = T - Tc = \$4 - \$1 = \$3$ per pair. Total taxes paid by producers = 150 x 3 = $450. Net price received by producers (producers' supply price) = $P_0 - Tp = \$50 - \$3 = \$47$. Total Tax Revenue collected by the government = 150 x $4 = $600

Confirm that the buyers pay $Tc = \$3$ and producers pay $Tp = \$1$ in market model B where demand is relatively inelastic. Confirm that the buyers pay $Tc = \$4$ and producers pay

55

Tp = $0 in market model C where demand is perfectly inelastic. From this example you can see that when demand is elastic, the producers bear the greatest burden of the tax and therefore receive a lower net price. If demand is inelastic, buyers bear the greatest burden of tax and producers receive a bigger net price. Who bears the greatest burden of a tax when demand is perfectly elastic?

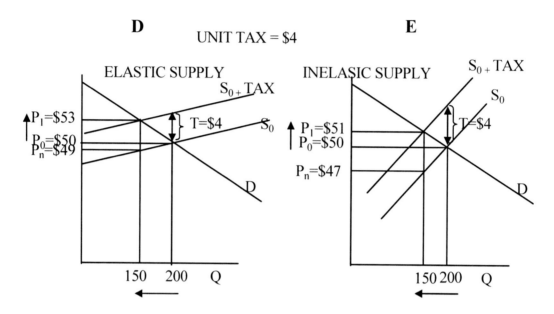

D   UNIT TAX = $4   **E**

b) Supply elasticity and the tax incidence.

In market model D, where supply is elastic, the buyers bear the greatest burden of the tax and the sellers receive a big net price of ($49). In market model E, where supply is inelastic, the producers bear the greatest burden of the tax and they receive a small net price of ($47).

Economic terms to remember:

Elasticity of demand	Inelastic demand	Elastic demand
Perfectly elastic	Perfectly inelastic	Arc elasticity of demand
Unit elasticity	Cross elasticity of demand	Income elasticity of demand
Elasticity of supply	The incidence of a tax	A normal good
An inferior good		

HOMEWWORK ON ELASTISITY

1. Complete columns C, D, E, and F, in the following table when prices **fall** from 48 to 40, 32 to 24, 16 to 8.

A	B	C	D	E	F
PRICE PER UNIT	TOTAL OTPUT	TR	DIRECTION OF TR CHANGE	THE COEFFICIENT OF PRICE ELASTICITY	CONCLUSION
48	32	---------			
40	36	---------	-----------	-----------	-----------
32	40	---------			
24	44	---------	-----------	-----------	-----------
16	48	---------			
8	52	---------	-----------	-----------	-----------

C=Total Revenue, D=whether increase, decrease or no change in Total Revenue, E=price elasticity of demand, F=whether elastic, inelastic or unitary elasticity. **Please use the arc elasticity (mid-point) formula to calculate elasticity of demand (column E)**

2) What happens to the size (absolute value) of the price elasticity coefficient as you move from right to left along a normal demand curve? (i.e. does it increase or decrease?)

3) Describe the relationship between elasticity of demand, price and total revenue. **(Please be thorough)**

4) When consumer incomes increased by 0.2%, quantity demanded for good X increased by 0.1%.
   a) What is the income elasticity of demand for good X?.......
   b) Is good X a necessity or a luxury?.......................
   c) How do you know whether it is a necessity or a luxury? (Be technical)..........................

5) A 5% reduction in the price of good Z results in 1.5% increase in the quantity demanded of good K.
   a) What is the cross elasticity of demand for the two goods..
   b) Are the two goods compliments or substitutes?.............
   c) How can you tell whether the two goods are substitutes or compliments? (Be technical)...............

6) Fitchburg Biker reduced its price for bicycles from $150.00 to $100.00 and bicycle sales increased from 300 to 500 a month.
   a) Compute Biker's price elasticity of demand.
   b) Was there a benefit in reducing price?
   c) Should Biker continue reducing price? e) Why?

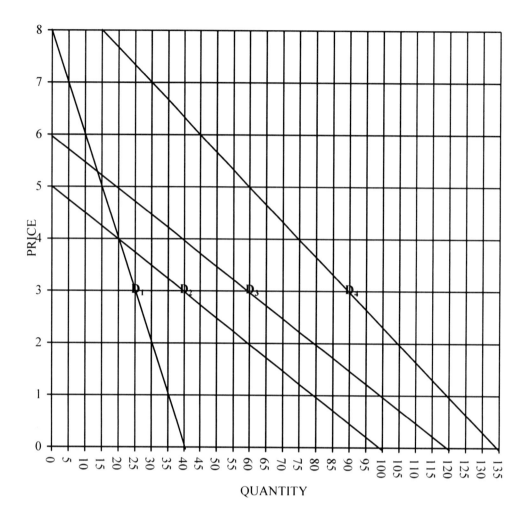

7) a) Calculate the arc price elasticity of demand (E_d) for D_1, D_2, D_3 and D_4 as price falls from $4 to $2 in the above diagram.

    i) D_1.........

    ii) D_2.........

    iii) D_3.........

    iv) D_4...............

b) Describe the elasticity for D_1, D_2 and D_3 and D_4? (i.e. whether elastic, inelastic or unitary)

    i) D_1...............

    ii) D^2...............

    iii) D_3...............

    iv) D_4.............

8) a) Use the following demand function to compute the coefficients of elasticity of demand at point A, B, C, and D.
   b) Compute total sales revenues (TR) at point A, B, C, and D.
   c) What conclusion do you draw about the relationship between total revenue and elasticity of demand?

Demand function: P = 5 – ½ Q

   $$Q = 10 – 2P$$

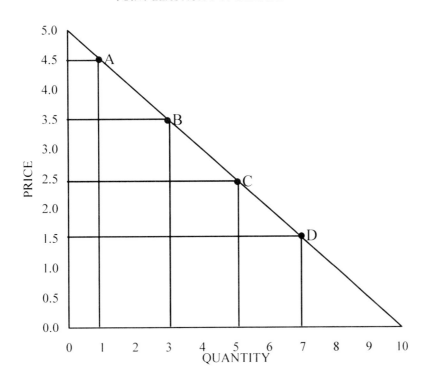

POINT ELASTICITY OF DEMAND

CHAPTER 5: PRODUCTION AND COSTS

The important question of **how** to produce (production planning) we encountered in chapter one, can be addressed through a production function.

A production function is a table, a graph or an equation showing the relationship between the maximum amounts of output that can be produced with a given number of inputs. It is constructed for a given time period and by assuming that there is a given level of technology that is known and fixed and also that resources are being fully utilized. The production function can be arrived at through some learning experience (learning curve). In this case a producer, through experience, can come to some conclusion about some input mix and the maximum output they would produce. It can also be determined prospectively through a planning process. It can be constructed with one variable input or many variable inputs.

The following are examples of production functions.

E.g.: $Q = f$ (Capital, Labor, Land, Energy etc.)
   OR $Q = f$ (Capital, Labor), $Q = f(K, L)$

where: Q = Output, K = Capital, L = Labor

Specifically: $Q = 2KL$ or $Q = 4K^{.5}L^{.4}$

The above functions define the maximum amount of output that can be produced with a given number of inputs. These examples imply that if the quantity of resources (inputs) is increased, output will increase and if they are reduced output (Q) will fall.

The costs of resources and the productivity of resources determine the number of resources used. Indirectly, then, the costs of production are a big determinant of output. The table and the graph below show the behavior of a short-run hypothetical production function when other factors are fixed and only one factor (labor) is varied. Note how output increases as the amount of labor increases and then decreases after the eleventh unit of labor is used.

The third column depicts the Average Product of Labor (APL).

The Average Product of Labor is a measure of the output produced per unit of input. This output per worker, or labor productivity as it is sometimes called, is calculated by using the following formula:

$$APL = \frac{TOTAL\ OUTPUT}{UNITS\ OF\ LABOR} = \frac{Q}{L}$$

Note also how the APL initially increases and then decreases. It decreases after the ninth unit of labor is used.

Economists are mostly interested in the fourth column that depicts the Marginal Product of labor (MPL). The Marginal Product of labor is the contribution of an extra unit of labor to total production. Geometrically, the MPL is the slope of the production function and it is calculated by using the following formula:

$$MPL = \frac{\text{CHANGE IN OUPUT}}{\text{CHANGE IN LABOR}} = \frac{\Delta Q}{\Delta L}$$

Note also how the MPL initially increases and then decreases. It decreases after the seventh unit of labor is used.

UNITS OF LABOR	TOTAL PRODUCT (Q)	AVERAGE PRODUCT (APL)	MARGINAL PRODUCT (MPL)
0	0	-	-
1	7	7.0	7
2	23	11.5	16
3	46	15.3	23
4	74	18.5	28
5	105	21.0	31
6	136	22.7	31
7	164	23.4	28
8	187	23.4	23
9	203	22.6	16
10	210	21.0	7
11	205	18.6	-5
12	185	15.4	-20

PRODUCTION FUNCTION

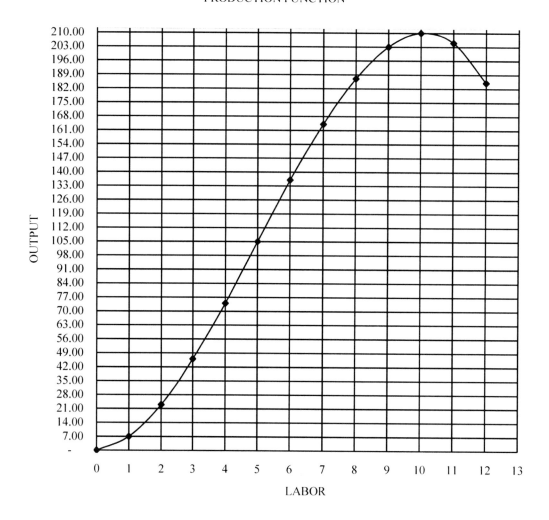

The above table and graph show that the contribution of one unit of labor to total production (marginal product of labor) increases up to the fifth unit and then it stays the same at the sixth unit and decreases after that and will become negative after the tenth unit. The function increases at an increasing rate (MPL is rising) up to the fifth unit and after that it increases at a decreasing rate (MPL is falling) up to the tenth unit of labor. At the maximum, the rate of change is zero. This type of production function is subject to the law of diminishing marginal returns also called the law of variable proportions.

DEFINITIONS OF CONCEPTS ASSOCIATED WITH PRODUCTION AND COSTS

THE LAW OF DIMINISHING MARGINAL RETURNS (DIMINISHING RETURNS)

The law of diminishing returns states that if you keep other factors of production fixed and then increase (vary) one factor, eventually the marginal product of the variable factor will decline (diminish). The law of diminishing returns is a short run phenomenon. Let us take the example of a farmer who has five acres of land and one tractor to use for her farming activities. Land and the tractor are the fixed inputs and labor is the variable input. If she starts with one person and successively increases the amount of labor, the law of diminishing returns says that, at some point total output will start to increase at a decreasing rate. Each additional worker contributes less and less to total output as workers get in each other's way and there is less land and capital equipment (one tractor) to work with. We shall discuss how the law of diminishing returns affects costs of production very shortly.

SHORT RUN---- The longest period of time during which **at least one factor (input) cannot be changed**. (A planning period over which at least one factor remains fixed)

LONG RUN---- The shortest period of time required to alter **all inputs**. (A planning period long enough to change all factors of production)

PRODUCTION COSTS

Explicit costs

Explicit costs are direct money outlays that must be paid. E.g. rent, wages, and cost of raw materials

Implicit costs

Implicit costs are opportunity costs for owner supplied capital or owner supplied labor. A businessperson incurs an opportunity cost if she uses her own resources, for example personal savings, in her business or works in her business full time instead of working for somebody else.

Opportunity cost of capital

The opportunity cost of capital is the amount that must be paid to an investor to induce investment in a business It is also called a normal rate of return

Fixed costs

Fixed costs (sunk costs) are costs that do not change with the level of output. Examples of fixed costs are rent; interest on debt; property taxes; insurance premiums; and **opportunity cost of capital and owner supplied inputs.** Fixed costs may have to be paid in the short run even if production does not take place

Variable costs

Variable costs are costs that change as output changes. Examples of variable costs are costs of raw materials; energy; and wages.

COMPUTING COSTS

1) TOTAL COST = TOTAL FIXED COSTS + TOTAL VARIABLE COSTS

$$TC = TFC + TVC$$

2) $TFC = TC - TVC$

3) $TVC = TC - TFC$

4) $\text{AVERAGE TOTAL COST} = \dfrac{\text{TOTAL COST}}{\text{OUTPUT}}$

4) $ATC = \dfrac{TC}{Q}$

4) $ATC = \dfrac{TC}{Q} = \dfrac{TFC}{Q} + \dfrac{TVC}{Q}$

5) $\text{AVERAGE VARIABLE COST} = \dfrac{\text{TOTAL VARIABLE COST}}{\text{OUTPUT}}$

5) $AVC = \dfrac{TVC}{Q}$

6) $\text{AVERAGE FIXED COST} = \dfrac{\text{TOTAL FIXED COST}}{\text{OUTPUT}}$

6) $AFC = \dfrac{TFC}{Q}$

7) $\text{MARGINAL COST} = \dfrac{\text{CHANGE IN TOTAL COST}}{\text{CHANGE IN OUTPUT}}$

7) $MC = \dfrac{\Delta TC}{\Delta Q}$

Marginal cost (MC) is the cost incurred as a result of producing an additional unit of output. It is the contribution to total costs by an extra unit of output.

THE SHUTDOWN RULE

The shutdown rule states that a firm should shut down (not exit) its operations in the **short run** if its _total revenue_ is less than its **total variable costs**

i.e. If TR < TVC or P < AVC-----shut down in the short run

If TR >TVC or P > AVC----continue production.

If TR > TVC, it means there is a contribution margin to fixed costs and therefore the firm should continue production. However, a firm should shutdown in the long run if TR < TC.

Should the firm, whose cost and revenue structures are shown below, shutdown in the short run?

TR = $60,000, TVC = 40,000, TFC = 30,000, TC = 70, 000

	SHUT DOWN	STAY OPEN
TR = $60,000	TR = 0	TR = $60,000
TVC = $40,000	TVC = 0	TVC = $40,000
TFC = $30,000	TC = TFC = $30,000	TFC = $30,000
TC = $70,000	PROFIT = -$30,000	PROFIT = -$10,000

It pays the firm to stay open in the short run because total revenue exceeds total variable cost by $20,000. The $20,000, over and above the variable costs, goes towards covering part of the total fixed costs. That is why it is called a contribution margin. Another way of looking at this is that the firm would lose $20,000 more by shutting down than by staying open.

PRODUCTIVITY AND SHORT RUN AND LONG RUN AVERAGE COSTS

If you look in any microeconomics textbook you will notice that the short run average cost curve is U-shaped. In the short run, as we have previously seen, a production unit may initially experience increasing marginal returns and then diminishing marginal returns to a variable factor. As more units of a factor are employed, a producer will incur more costs. We called these costs variable costs. The total variable costs will initially increase at a decreasing rate as output increases and then increase at an increasing rate because of the law of diminishing returns. This means that marginal cost will decrease and then increase. Similarly, average variable costs will decrease and then increase. As marginal productivity increases, smaller and smaller amounts of an input will be required to produce an extra unit of output and, assuming the same cost for every input used, the cost of producing an extra unit of output (marginal cost) and the average variable cost will become smaller and smaller. As marginal productivity falls, more and more inputs will be required to produce an extra unit of output and therefore marginal cost will rise and so will the average variable cost.

In the long run all factors are variable. A firm can choose the scale of production it wants. The shape of the long run average cost curve depends on how costs change as the scale of operation is changed. As the scale of production is increased, the production process may experience increasing returns to scale or decreasing returns to scale or constant returns to scale.

INCREASING RETURNS TO SCALE OR ECONOMIES OF LARGE SCALE PRODUCTION (ECONOMIES OF SCALE)

You have increasing returns to scale if a certain percentage **increase** in all inputs (factors) leads to a greater percentage **increase** in output. A 20% increase in inputs, for example, leads to 30% increase in output. Increasing returns to scale is a long run phenomenon. (Why?) Increasing returns to scale occur because of specialization. With increasing output, labor becomes specialized and plant and equipment can be used efficiently. This will lead to lower average costs for every unit of output produced. The firm's average total cost curve will be downward sloping. Increasing returns to scale may act as barriers to entry in an industry because small firms whose start-up costs are high may not compete effectively.

TYPES OF ECONOMIES OF SCALE:
a) Plant economies (efficient capital)
Large-scale production leads to the efficient use of big machines.
Low levels of output will mean that some machines will stay idle and small versions of some machines may be uneconomical to use. A farmer with five acres of land, one tractor and one helper will not keep the tractor and his helper fully occupied because her operation is small. In this case the unit costs will be too high to justify the use of these resources. At the same time you cannot design a small tractor to cultivate just five acres of land, as this would be uneconomical. If a car assembly line was used to produce ten cars a week instead of say five hundred cars it is capable of producing when operating at full capacity, the average cost of producing ten cars would be higher than the cost for producing five hundred. Again a small assembly line to produce only five cars will be uneconomical.
A day care center that has two rooms and two teachers may cater for five kids or twenty kids. With five kids, however, the cost of providing care per child will be higher than the cost for twenty kids because the cost of electricity, heating, salaries and general maintenance is the same whether you have five kids or twenty kids. You cannot construct a very small room just for five kids as this may be uneconomical and may not meet the minimum standards required by law. For most production processes there is a certain minimum efficient plant size below which you cannot operate efficiently.

b) Labor economies (labor specialization)
Large-scale production leads to labor specialization. This way labor becomes skilled, efficient, and more productive thus leading to lower costs of production.
c) Financial economies
Big businesses are able to finance their businesses more easily and at a lower cost than small businesses because they deal in big volumes, which lead to lower transaction costs. Big businesses also have less risk with a lot of collateral. This is why you have the prime interest rate (prime rate). The prime rate is given to the banks' best customers.
d) Marketing economies

Large firms can buy and sell at a discount and have ability to advertise their products.

From the previous discussion, you can see that economies of scale are associated with savings in business costs because of size.

DECREASING RETURNS TO SCALE OR DISECONOMIES OF SCALE

You have decreasing returns to scale if a certain percentage **increase** in all inputs (factors) leads to a smaller percentage **increase** in output. A 20% increase in inputs will lead to a 10% increase in output. It is also a long run phenomenon that results in higher average costs per unit. As the firm becomes big there may be problems of coordination and management that lead to inefficiency and higher production costs.

CONSTANT RETURNS TO SCALE

A production unit experiences constant returns to scale when a certain percentage **increase** in inputs (factors) leads to the same percentage **increase** in output. Ex. increase inputs by 20%, output increases by 20%. The concept is associated with constant ATCs.

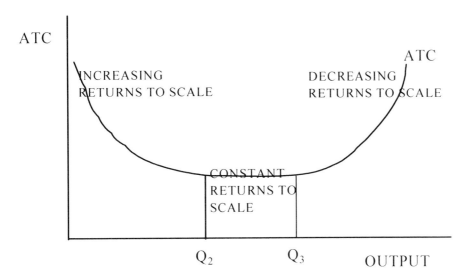

COMPUTING REVENUE

At this point, let us also define the revenue concepts formally before we discuss the role of revenue and costs in the production decision making of business firms.

1) TOTAL REVENUE = PRICE x QUANTITY

1)   TR   =   P x Q

2) AVERAGE REVENUE = $\dfrac{\text{TOTAL REVENUE}}{\text{OUTPUT}}$ = PRICE

2) AR = $\dfrac{TR}{Q}$ = $\dfrac{PQ}{Q}$ = P

3) MARGINAL REVENUE $= \dfrac{\text{CHANGE IN TOTAL REVENUE}}{\text{CHANGE IN OUTPUT}}$

3) $MR = \dfrac{\Delta TR}{\Delta Q}$

Marginal revenue is the revenue associated with selling an additional unit of output. It is the contribution of an extra unit of output to total sales revenue.

Economic terms to remember:

Implicit costs	Fixed costs
Explicit costs	Variable costs
Opportunity cost	Marginal cost
Increasing returns to scale	Economies of scale
Marginal revenue	Decreasing returns to scale
Constant returns to scale	Diminishing marginal returns

HOMEWORK ON COSTS:

Complete the following two tables

OUTPUT	TFC $	TVC $	TC $	MC $	AVC $	AFC $	ATC $
0			10.00	-	-	-	-
1							38.10
2					26.4	5.00	
3		74.70		21.90			
4							26.1
5					22.50		
6			139.60				

TFC=TOTAL FIXED COST; TVC=TOTAL VARIABLE COST; TC=TOTAL COST;
MC=MARGINAL COST; AVC=AVERAGE VARIABLE COST;
AFC=AVERAGE FIXED COST; ATC=AVERAGE TOTAL COST;

OUTPUT	TFC $	TVC $	TC $	MC $	AVC $	AFC $	ATC $
0			500	-	-	-	-
1			600				
2			700				
3			800				
4			900				
5			1000				
6			1100				

TFC=TOTAL FIXED COST; TVC=TOTAL VARIABLE COST; TC=TOTAL COST;
MC=MARGINAL COST; AVC=AVERAGE VARIABLE COST;
AFC=AVERAGE FIXED COST; ATC=AVERAGE TOTAL COST

CHAPTER 6: PERFECT COMPETITION (THE IDEAL MARKET)

The market we referred to in chapter two, where prices are determined by the forces of supply and demand, is called a perfectly competitive market.

THE CHARACTERISTICS OF PERFECT COMPETITION

The following conditions are required for a competitive market to exist:

1) Very many sellers and buyers

There should be a large number of independent sellers (firms) and buyers to have meaningful competition in the market. The firms are assumed to be relatively small in size so that they cannot individually influence the market price. The buyers also cannot individually influence the market price.

2) A standardized (homogeneous) product

The firms are assumed to be producing products that are indistinguishable from one another (identical products) so that consumers are indifferent as to what product they buy. If this condition is satisfied, sellers cannot charge different prices and competition will be reinforced.

3) Free entry and exit (no blocked entry)

Free entry means that anyone can enter the industry and produce without facing many obstacles like high set-up costs, government licenses, high advertising expenses, and other barriers from other businesses. Free entry is an important condition because without it, the industry will have few players and therefore become less competitive. Free entry ensures that when profits are made in the industry, new firms will enter to compete for profits therefore increase supply and bring the market price down.

Freedom of exit is also necessary because if it is costly to exit, then firms may not enter in the first place. Industries with heavy capital equipment and high sunk costs are difficult to enter and exit. It is costly to enter such industries because of high set up costs and consequently it is not easy to leave the industry without incurring much loss. In the long run firms should be able to leave the industry if they are incurring losses and move their capital to where it is profitable.

4) Perfect information about product prices, product quality and input prices

Buyers must have equal access to information on product prices, product quality, and the location of the product. Given that the products are homogeneous, and there are many sellers of these products, no single seller will have power on the price of the product as long as buyers have equal access to information.

This will make competition thrive. Likewise, sellers must have equal access to information about input prices, their quality, their availability, and the level of technology. As we shall see later, the above condition is the most difficult to satisfy because information is costly.

5) Perfect mobility of factors of production

Factor mobility is the ability of factors of production to move from one function to another or place to place at minimum cost. Factors must be mobile both geographically and occupationally to reinforce the condition of free entry
and guarantee large numbers and therefore enhance competition.

AN INDIVIDUAL FIRM IN A PERFECTLY COMPETITIVE MARKET

A firm operating under the above conditions has no market power.

The firm cannot, through its actions, control price because it contributes a very small proportion to the total industry output. This is so because there are many sellers selling a homogeneous product and the buyers have all the necessary information about the quality and price of the product. The price is determined by the whole industry through the forces of supply and demand and the firm sells at that price. The firm, therefore, becomes a price taker. The firm faces a perfectly elastic demand curve for its product. This means that if it were to increase price on its own, it could not sell anything since buyers know the existence, location, and prices of other identical products. If the firm lowered the price, it would probably sell everything. This would be irrational, though, since a higher price is being offered in the market and the firm can sell all it wants at the market price.

The diagram below shows that a firm will sell 10 units at the price of $10 determined by the market through supply and demand.

THE FIRM VIS-A-VIS THE MARKET (INDUSTRY)

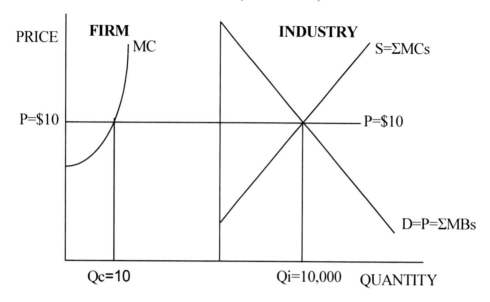

P = Price
MC = Marginal Cost
S = Supply = ΣMCs[10]
D = Demand = ΣMBs
ΣMCs = Sum of Marginal Costs
ΣMBs = Sum of Marginal Benefits
Qc = Firm's output
Qi = Industry output
Note: The two diagrams above are not drawn to scale.

The firm represented in the above diagram will have the following revenue function: TR = PQ = 10Q. You will observe from the table and the graph below that a firm that sells at a fixed price per unit of output, its price (average revenue) is equal to its marginal revenue. Go back to the section titled 'Computing Revenue' and confirm the information given in the table below.

What does 10 represent in the function TR = 10Q?

TR = PQ = 10Q				
QUANTITY	TOTAL REVENUE	PRICE	AVERAGE REVENUE	MARGINAL REVENUE
0	0	-	-	-
1	10	10	10	10
2	20	10	10	10
3	30	10	10	10
4	40	10	10	10

---

[10] See the discussion on the derivation of the market supply curve at the end of this chapter and the derivation of the market demand curve in chapter 3.

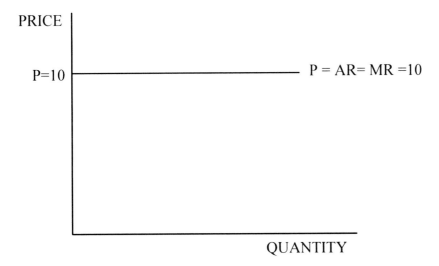

PRICE

P=10 ——————————————————— P = AR= MR =10

QUANTITY

PROFIT MAXIMIZATION AND OUTPUT DETERMINATION

A firm, in a competitive market, will produce the level of output that maximizes profits. At the profits maximizing level of output, total revenue exceeds total cost by the greatest amount and it follows that at the profit maximizing level of output, **marginal cost** is equal to **marginal revenue.** The necessary condition for profit maximization is that marginal cost must be equal to marginal revenue. This, however, is not a sufficient condition. The sufficient condition is that marginal cost must be rising at the profit maximizing level of output. These two conditions must be satisfied to determine the level of output that maximizes profits.

TOTAL REVENUE AND TOTAL COST
APPROACH TO PROFIT MAXIMIZATION

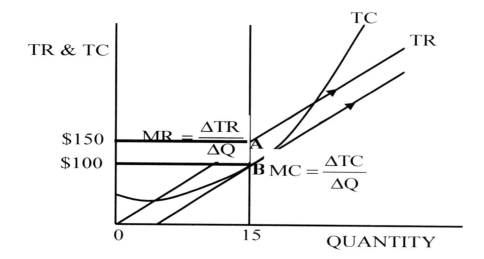

The difference between TR and TC (profit) will be highest at the output
of 15. Note that a parallel line to the TR line is also a tangent to the TC curve at the output
of 15 (point B). This can happen only at one point. At any other point of tangency, the line
cannot be parallel to the TR curve and therefore TR will exceed TC by a lower amount
than at point B. When two lines are parallel to each other, their slopes are equal. The slope
of the TC curve (MC) is equal to the slope of the TR curve (MR) at the output of 15 and
profits are maximized at that point.

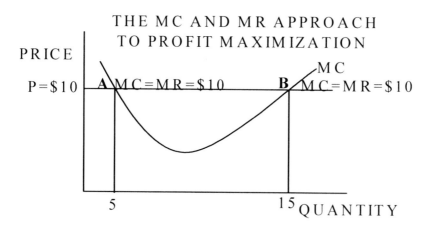

At the output of 5 units (point A), MC = MR but also at the output of 15 (point B),
MC = MR. Which output maximizes profits? It cannot be 5 because every unit from 6 to
15 adds more to revenue than it adds to cost (i.e. P>MC). After 15 units, every unit of
output adds more to cost than it adds to revenue
(i.e. P<MC). At 15, MC = MR and MC is also rising. Both conditions for profit
maximization are satisfied at that point.

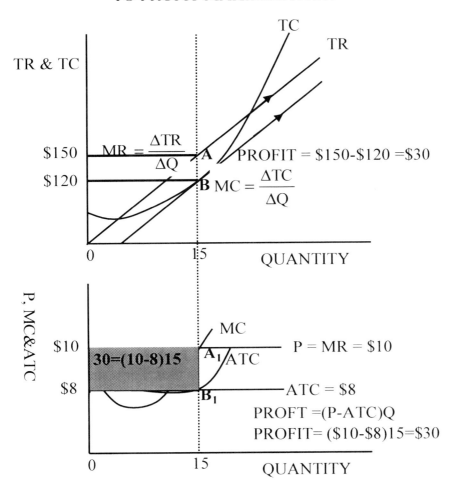

TR&TC, MR&MC APPROACH
TO PROFIT MAXIMIZATION

PROFITS

    If Total Revenue is greater than Total Cost (TR - TC > 0), a firm earns abnormal profits in the short run. If Total Revenue is equal to Total Cost (TR - TC = 0), a firm earns a normal profit (a normal rate of return)[11]. It is called a normal rate of return because the firm covers its opportunity cost at that point. If Total Revenue is less than Total Cost (TR - TC < 0), a firm incurs an economic loss.

---

[11] See the following discussion on profit

ACCOUNTING PROFITS VERSUS ECONOMIC PROFITS

When computing profits accountants compute profits by getting the difference between explicit costs and the revenue generated by the firm. This is what is reported on financial statements. Economists, on the other hand, are interested in the difference between revenue and all costs i.e. explicit and implicit costs. Implicit costs you will recall are associated with the opportunity cost of owner-supplied capital and owner-supplied labor. In other words it is the opportunity cost of the resources a firm already owns. These do not appear on the financial records because the firm does not make direct payments for their use. Let us take an example of a mechanic who sets up her own business to repair and service cars. She uses her own building for her operations, uses her life savings to start the business, and works in her shop fifty hours a week. If the building could be used for other functions then there is an opportunity cost for its use in the current business. There is implicit rent that the building could otherwise fetch. By using her savings and her own labor, she forgoes interest payments that would accrue from alternative investment and forgoes wages she would have received by working for somebody else. Let us suppose that the alternative wage is estimated to be $33,600 a year, forgone interest is $400 a year and forgone rent is $6,000 a year. The opportunity cost would amount to $40,000 a year.

Opportunity costs are difficult to determine but economists insist that they must be estimated and taken into account. The firm must, at the very least, earn a return equal to its opportunity cost. This type of return is called a normal return or a normal profit and in essence it is an implicit cost because it is a return that a firm would have earned if it had chosen to invest it resources in some alternative enterprise. It is a return required to keep the resources of the entrepreneur (the mechanic) employed in their present production activities or else they will be moved to other more productive uses. For a small business, the normal return would be equivalent to the interest rate on risk-free government bonds or certificates of deposit.

For a big enterprise that requires external financing, the investors must be kept happy also by receiving a rate of return that is greater than they would otherwise receive from alternative investments. Economists are interested in economic profits because they are used to evaluate business performance and make economic decisions. If a firm is earning a normal return it will continue with its current operations. If the return were below normal, then it would be difficult for the firm to raise needed capital and the firm may cease its current operations and do something else. If the return is above normal new capital and new firms will be attracted into the industry and there will be an inducement for old firms to expand.

FIRM A	
ACCOUNTING PROFITS	ECONOMIC PROFITS
TFC = 80,000	TFC = 80,000 + 40,000 (OPPORTUNITY COST) = 120,000
TVC = 120,000	TVC = 120,000
TC = 200,000	TC = 240,000
TR = 240,000	TR = 240,000
PROFIT = TR – TC = 40,000	PROFIT = TR – TC = 0

FIRM B	
ACCOUNTING PROFITS	ECONOMIC PROFITS
TFC = 60,000	TFC = 60,000 + 20,000 (OPPORTUNITY COST) TFC = 80,000
TVC = 100,000	TVC = 100,000
TC = 160,000	TC = 180,000
TR = 220,000	TR = 220,000
PROFIT = TR – TC = 60,000	PROFIT = TR – TC = 40,000

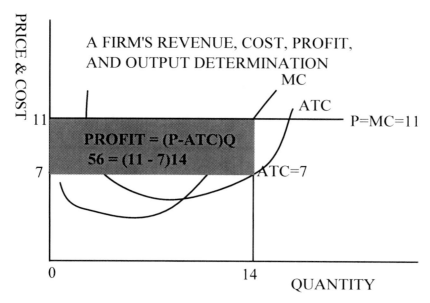

A FIRM'S REVENUE, COST, PROFIT,
AND OUTPUT DETERMINATION

A competitive firm, whose revenue and cost structures are depicted in the above diagram, will produce 14 units of output in order to maximize profits.

At that level of output marginal revenue is equal to marginal cost. Each unit will be produced at an average cost (ATC) of $7. The firm will earn a profit of $56 as shown in above diagram and the table below.

PRICE	QUANTITY	TR = PxQ	TC=ATCxQ	PROFIT=TR-TC
$11	14	$11x14 = $154	$7x14 = $98	$154-$98 = $56

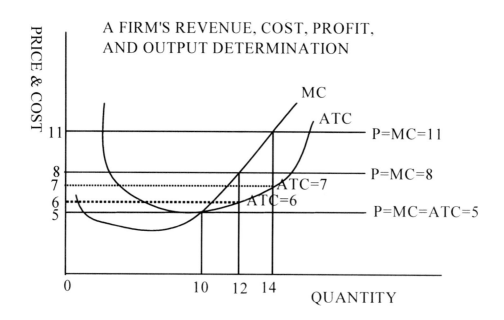

A FIRM'S REVENUE, COST, PROFIT,
AND OUTPUT DETERMINATION

The above graph and the following table show the units that would be produced at various prices. At the market price of $11 we have already seen that 14 units will be produced. The average cost of producing 14 units is $7. At the price of $8, 12 units of output will be supplied and the average cost of producing them will be $6. At the price $5 per unit, 10 units will be supplied and each unit will be produced at the cost of $5 per unit. See the table below for revenue, cost, and profit.

PRICE	QUANTITY	TR = PxQ	TC=ATCxQ	PROFIT=TR-TC
$11	14	$11x14 = $154	$7x14 = $98	$154-$98 = $56
$8	12	$8x12 = $96	$6x12 = $72	$96-$72 = $24
$5	10	$5x10 = $50	$5x10 = $50	$50-$50 = $0

THREE POSSIBLE PROFIT SITUATIONS IN THE SHORT RUN

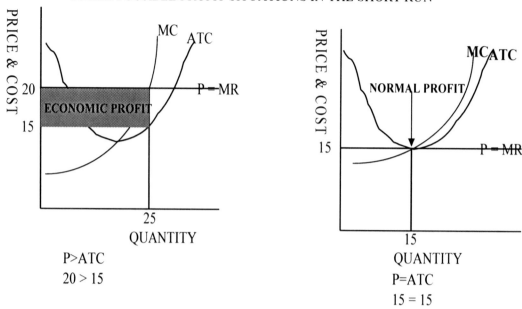

P>ATC
20 > 15

P=ATC
15 = 15

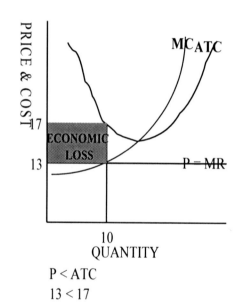

P < ATC
13 < 17

THE MARKET SYSTEM AND OUTPUT DETERMINATION

Given the profit motive, those products that give a higher return will attract a lot of resources and will therefore be produced. If demand is high and the industry is earning an abnormal return, other producers will be attracted to the industry and resources will flow to the profitable industry because there are no barriers to entry and resources are assumed to be mobile. As more firms enter the industry and old firms expand, supply in the market will increase relative to demand. This process will eventually lead to lower prices in the market and the excessive profits will be competed away. The industry will be operating in what is called a long-run equilibrium where **most firms** earn **a** normal return.

A normal return is earned when the price of a product is equal to the average total cost (P = ATC).

There will be a few firms whose average total costs are greater than price (ATC>P) and these will be forced to exit the industry. There will also be some few firms whose average total costs are less than market price (ATC<P) and these firms will earn economic rent. Economic rent is a return earned by a resource in fixed supply or a resource with special attributes. It is a return over and above what is required to keep the resource in its current use. Major league athletes, singers, movie stars, writers earn economic rent.

There are two important market outcomes of these market adjustments.

The largest possible output will be produced and supplied at a lower price and every firm will produce at the lowest cost possible to earn a normal return and survive.

The following graph shows how the industry and the firm may adjust from the short run to the long run.

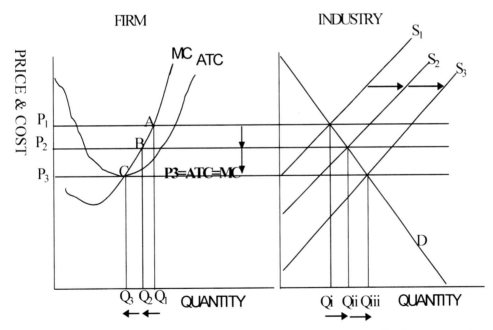

The firm will continuously adjust its output to keep its marginal cost equal to price and Q_3 will be the representative firm's long run equilibrium output and Qiii will be the industry's long run equilibrium output.

LONG RUN SITUATIONS

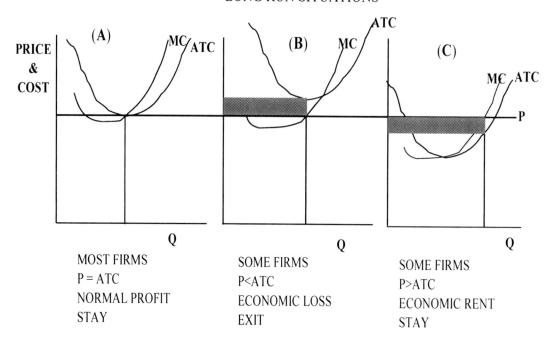

Firm A in the above diagram depicts a typical long run situation for most firms in a competitive industry. There still will be some firms, depicted by firm C that will earn economic rent because they have specialized factors of production. Since this is a highly competitive market, some firms will compete for these factors so that they can enjoy the economic rents. The rents will thus represent a cost to whoever is successful in buying these factors. This will push up their average total costs and they will earn a normal return like everybody else. If the owner does not choose to sell, she must pay the factors an economic rent to be able to retain them. This will increase her costs again leading to a normal profit. In the long run most firms will earn a normal return so that there is no incentive to either enter or leave the industry.

THE FIRM'S SHORTRUN AND LONG RUN SUPPLY CURVE

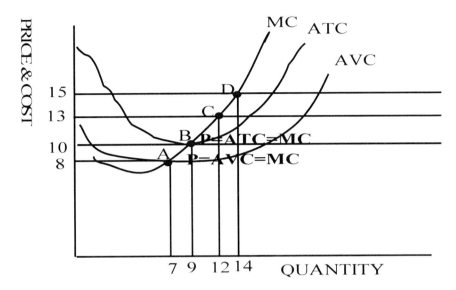

The **short run supply curve** of the firm is the marginal cost curve above the average variable cost (AVC) curve. In the above case, 7 units will be supplied at the price of $8, 9 units at the price of $10, 12 units at the price of $13, and 14 units at the price of $15. More units will be supplied at a price above the price of $15.

The price of $8, where P = MC =AVC, is called the short run shutdown price. It is the point below which the firm will have to shut down in the short run. It will have to shut down because below that point, price will be less than average variable cost (AVC), i.e. total revenue (TR) will be less than total variable cost (TVC).

The **long run supply curve** of the firm is the marginal cost curve above the average total cost (ATC) curve. In the above case, 9 units will be supplied at the price of $10, 12 units at the price of $13, and 14 units at the price of $15. More units will be supplied at any price above the price of $15. The price of $10, where P = MC = ATC, is called the long run shutdown price. It is the point below which the firm will have to shut down in the long run. It will have to shut down because below that point, price will be less than average total cost (ATC), i.e. total revenue (TR) will be less than total cost (TC).

THE MARKET SUPPLY CURVE

We derive the market supply curve by adding the quantities that each individual firm is willing to sell at each price. The supply curve, in other words, is the horizontal summation of the marginal cost curves. You will recall that the firm's marginal cost curve, above its variable costs, is its supply curve. If these curves are combined together we get a market supply curve. In the example below, we use two firms to show how a market supply curve can be derived.

Firm A sells 5 units of output at the price of $4 and firm B sells 8 units at the same price. The total quantity supplied by the two firms at the price of $4 is 13 units. At a higher price of $ 6, firm A sells 7 units and firm B sells 11 units. The market total is 18. The process of deriving a market supply curve would be the same for any number of firms. The market supply curve (S) = the Sum of Marginal Costs = ΣMCs.

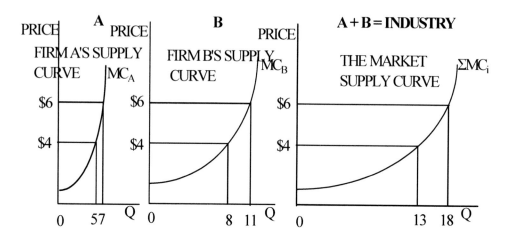

THE MARKET SYSTEM AND THE BASIC ECONOMIC PROBLEM

THE MARKET SYSTEM AND PRODUCTION PLANNING

The market will assign resources to firms that can make the most productive use of them. The most profitable firms will attract resources and unprofitable firms will be deprived. If demand for the product is high, a firm will earn abnormal profits and, as we indicated, new firms will be attracted in the industry and old firms will expand. This will increase demand for resources. The demand for resources is a **derived demand** in that it is from the products the resources help produce. In this case consumers will have revealed their preferences by demanding more and producers and resource owners will have responded to these market forces by supplying more. The producers will endeavor to produce at the lowest cost possible to remain competitive and therefore the market prices of resources and their productivity will be very important in determining how much resources are used and in what proportions.

THE MARKET SYSTEM AND THE DISTRIBUTION OF OUTPUT

If we take consumer tastes and preferences as given, ability and willingness to pay the current market price for the product will determine the distribution of the product to consumers. Ability to pay depends on the size of money income and wealth, and these depend on the amount of physical and human resources owned and their quality. Supply and demand of inputs in the input market, will determine the prices of labor (wages) and the prices of capital (interest). The higher the quality of resources, the greater the price they fetch in the market place, and the larger the money incomes the resource owners will have. People with more money incomes and wealth will have more goods and services and those with less income will have less goods and services. Thus the market rations the output according to people's ability and willingness to pay the equilibrium price. This is the market's answer to the question of who gets what and in what amounts paused earlier.

The accumulation of resources may depend on factors like hard work, entrepreneurship, luck and initial endowments.

THE MARKET SYSTEM AND ECONOMIC GROWTH

One of the functions of an economic system is to encourage economic growth. You have economic growth when more and better goods and services are produced thus leading to a higher standard of living. This may come about as a result of an increase in the quantity of resources, an increase in the quality of resources, an increase in population, improvement in technology, and more investments. What is the role of the price system in all this? When businesses expect high profits in the future, they will sacrifice consumption now and invest in research and development for the purposes of producing more goods and better goods. Other firms will do the same and with increased competition, more goods will be produced. We saw that in order for the firms in a competitive environment to survive and maintain abnormal profits, they must strive to introduce new technology and produce at the lowest costs possible. Households will also save more if they expect a higher return in the future. More savings will go to the production of capital goods and therefore increase the rate of economic growth.

In a market system, expectations of profit act as a big incentive for taking risks, investing and producing more. An increase in population may increase demand for goods and services and therefore increase their prices and this may also give an incentive for businesses to produce more.

THE VIRTUES OF THE MARKET SYSTEM: A SUMMARY

In a market system, firms achieve economic efficiency thereby allocating society's resources efficiently. It has been noted that a producer in a competitive market, maximizes profits by producing an output level where marginal cost is equal to price. This is precisely the condition for allocative efficiency we described earlier. For the entire industry, allocative efficiency is achieved at the equilibrium price. At this point the sum of marginal costs is equal to the sum of marginal benefits (i.e. supply is equal to demand).

Firms in a competitive market also achieve production efficiency by producing at the lowest cost. Competitive pressures force firms to produce at the lowest cost, improve the quality of their products and sell their products at lower prices. These competitive forces may lead to technological innovation, which may reduce costs and improve product quality even further. As prices are reduced and quality is improved, consumers buy more and more wants are satisfied as more goods are made available at a lower price. Personal computers (PCs), VCRs, CDs, digital watches, and hand-held calculators are good examples of products whose quality has improved and prices fallen due to competitive market forces.

Economic terms to remember:

A normal return	Allocative efficiency
Accounting profits	Derived demand
Economic efficiency	Economic profits
Economic rent	Marginal cost
Long run supply curve	Market supply curve

Marginal revenue
Production efficiency
Short run supply curve

Profits
Profit maximization

HOMEWORK ON PERFECT COMPETITION

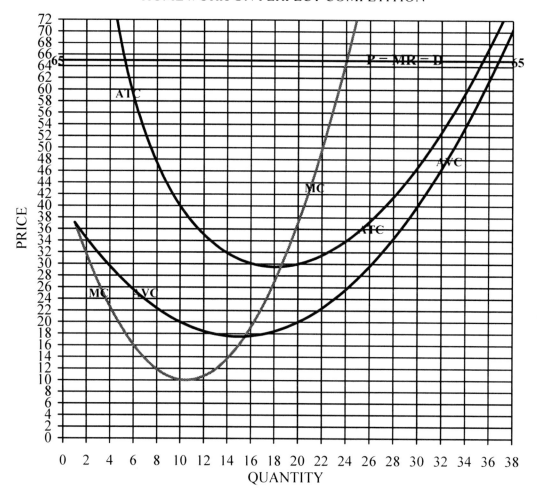

Use the above diagram to answer the following questions. (Assume the firm is a **profit maximizer** operating in a competitive market)

a) How many units of output will the firm produce and sell?.........

b) What is the total revenue (TR) at this level of output?..............

c) What is the total cost (TC) at this level of output?.................

d) What is the total profit at this level of output?...................

e) What is the average total cost (ATC) at this level of output?....

f) What is the total fixed cost (TFC) at this level of output?......

g) What is the total variable cost (TVC) at this level of output?..........

h) What is the average fixed cost (AFC) at this level of output?.........

i) What is the short run shut down price?...........................

OUTPUT	PRICE	AR	MR	MC	TR	TC	PROFIT
0					0.00	20.00	-20.00
1	37.00	37.00	37.00	38.10	37.00	58.10	-21.10
2	37.00	37.00	37.00	34.70	74.00	92.80	-18.80
3	37.00	37.00	37.00	31.90	111.00	124.70	-13.70
4	37.00	37.00	37.00	29.70	148.00	154.40	-6.40
5	37.00	37.00	37.00	28.10	185.00	182.50	2.50
6	37.00	37.00	37.00	27.10	222.00	209.60	12.40
7	37.00	37.00	37.00	26.70	259.00	236.30	22.70
8	37.00	37.00	37.00	26.90	296.00	263.20	32.80
9	37.00	37.00	37.00	27.70	333.00	290.90	42.10
10	37.00	37.00	37.00	29.10	370.00	320.00	50.00
11	37.00	37.00	37.00	31.10	407.00	351.10	55.90
12	37.00	37.00	37.00	33.70	444.00	384.80	59.20
13	37.00	37.00	37.00	36.90	481.00	421.70	59.30
14	37.00	37.00	37.00	40.70	518.00	462.40	55.60
15	37.00	37.00	37.00	45.10	555.00	507.50	47.50

a) Complete the columns for price, average revenue (AR), marginal revenue (MR), marginal cost (MC), and profit in the table above.

b) What is the amount of output that maximizes profits?

CHAPTER 7: MONOPOLY

A monopoly exists when a single firm supplies the entire market a product for which there are no close substitutes. Monopolies may arise because of technological superiority that lead to overwhelming economies of scale that results in lower unit costs. This may virtually prevent competitors from entering the industry.

There are monopolies that are sanctioned by the government for various reasons. For example monopolies may be allowed to exist because they provide a universal service that may not be provided 'fairly' by the private market. A post office is a good example of a firm that is perceived this way. The argument is that some remote rural areas may not be served by the private market if it is costly to do so or may be served at a higher cost than other places.

Some monopolies, known as natural monopolies, exist because the market can only support only one firm. A natural monopoly is a firm that supplies the entire market more efficiently than two or more firms would. These are characterized by the falling average costs for the entire demand range.

Most public utilities like electric companies, water and sewer companies, and gas companies fall in this category. Given the size of the market it may be efficient to have one electric company in some locality as more companies may lead to the duplication of capital.

Barriers to entry like economies of scale; patents; copyrights; control of resources; and government sanctions help monopolies to maintain their market power.

Monopolies face a downward sloping inelastic demand curve for their products, which implies that they have a high degree of market power. They are price makers rather than price takers.

If allowed to operate in their best interests, monopolists tend to charge a higher price and produce a less than a socially desirable output. In fact they charge a price which is greater than marginal cost thus under allocating society's resources.

The interests of monopolists are served when they maximize profits. They maximize profits by producing the level of output where marginal cost is equal to marginal revenue. When MC = MR, total revenue will exceed total cost by the greatest amount. At that point, however, marginal revenue is not equal to price (MC = MR ≠ P).

In fact marginal revenue is less than price because the demand curve (i.e. the price line) is downward sloping. Let us digress and discuss the relationship between price and marginal revenue for a monopolist.

Since a monopolist faces a downward sloping demand curve for her product, price must be lowered in order to sell more units. Let us say a monopolist starts by selling two units of output at the price of $4.50 per unit thus generating total revenue in the amount of $9.00. In order to sell three units the price has to drop to $4.25. The decrease in price affects marginal revenue in two distinct ways. One is a negative effect and another is positive. All the three units are now selling at a lower price of $4.25each and the total revenue is $12.75. Two units are selling less than previously. Specifically they are contributing $0.50 less ($0.25 each). If we deduct this from the previous revenue that was generated from selling two units of output we end up with ($9.00 – 0.50) = $8.50. $0.50 is a negative contribution resulting from the decrease in price. The third unit of course has a positive contribution of $4.25 (new price). The new revenue generated from the sale of three units is $12.75 ($8.50 + $4.25). The additional revenue (MR) resulting from lowering price to sell an extra unit of out put is $3.75 ($12.75 - $9.00) which is lower than the price of $4.75. Alternatively we can approach this by subtracting the loss in revenue from the gain in revenue ($4.25 - $0.50) to get the net gain in revenue (MR) of $3.75. As long as the demand curve is downward sloping, marginal revenue will be less than price.

When an additional unit is sold, total revenue may increase or decrease. This will depend on whether the negative effects outweigh the positive effects or the positive effects outweigh the negative effects.

Note the following facts about the relationship between marginal revenue and total revenue:[12]

a) As long as the demand curve is downward sloping, marginal revenue will be less than price.

b) Marginal revenue can either be positive or negative.

c) When marginal revenue is positive, total revenue will increase as output increases.

d) When marginal revenue is zero, total revenue will reach its maximum.

f) When marginal revenue is negative, total revenue will decrease as output increases.

[12] See the graph titled 'The Relationship between Elasticity of Demand, Marginal Revenue, and Total Revenue'. Note that the marginal revenue values on the said graph would be slightly different from the marginal revenue values calculated from a unit change in output because they are calculated for infinitesimal changes in output.

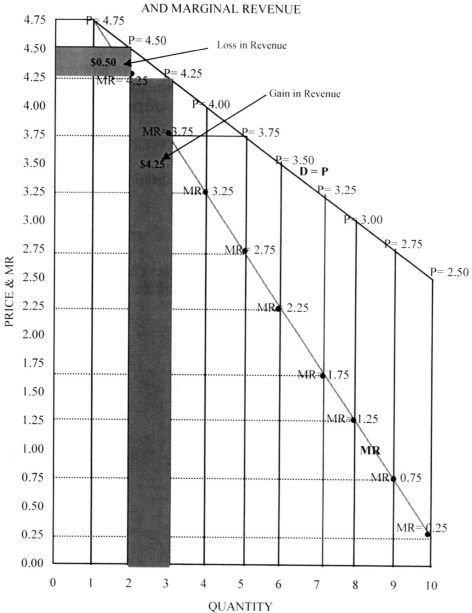

THE RELATIONSHIP BETWEEN PRICE
AND MARGINAL REVENUE

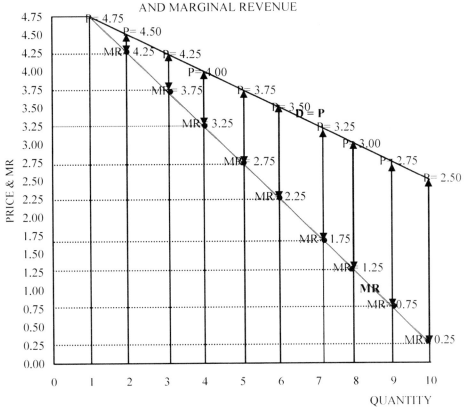

THE RELATIONSHIP BETWEEN PRICE
AND MARGINAL REVENUE

QUANTITY	TOTAL REVENUE	PRICE	MARGINAL REVENUE
1	$4.75	$4.75	$4.75
2	9.00	4.50	4.25
3	12.75	4.25	3.75
4	16.00	4.00	3.25
5	18.75	3.75	2.75
6	21.00	3.50	2.25
7	22.75	3.25	1.75
8	24.00	3.00	1.25
9	24.75	2.75	0.75
10	25.00	2.50	0.25

91

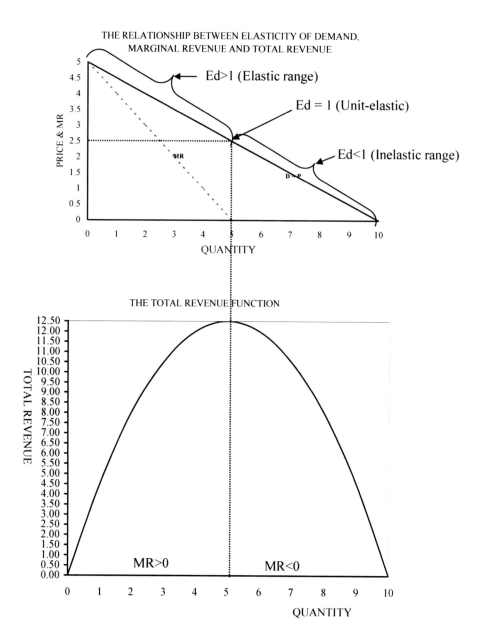

THE RELATIONSHIP BETWEEN ELASTICITY OF DEMAND,
MARGINAL REVENUE AND TOTAL REVENUE

Ed>1 (Elastic range)

Ed = 1 (Unit-elastic)

Ed<1 (Inelastic range)

MR

D = P

PRICE & MR

QUANTITY

THE TOTAL REVENUE FUNCTION

TOTAL REVENUE

MR>0

MR<0

QUANTITY

PRICE AND OUTPUT DETERMINATION BY A MONOPOLIST

We have already stated that a monopolist maximize profits by producing the level of output where marginal cost is equal to marginal revenue. Total revenue will exceed total cost by the greatest amount at that point. At the profit maximizing level of output MC = MR but MR is not equal to price. In so doing a monopolist produces less than the socially desirable output. The following diagrams illustrate how a monopolist determines price or output and the inefficiencies associated with a monopoly.

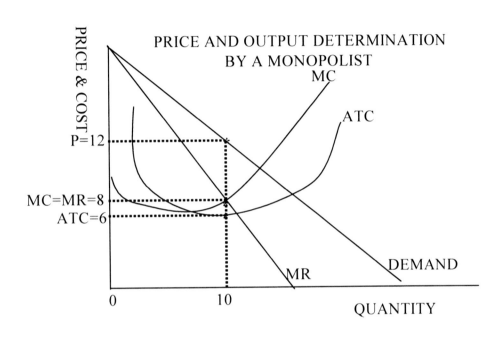

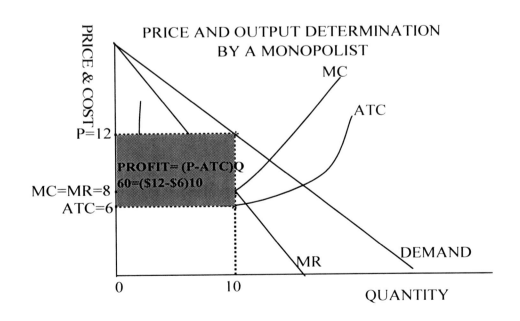

In the monopoly model above, 10 units of output will be produced and the price charged will be $12. This price is determined by the demand curve.

A monopolist can control either output or price but not both. If, for example, she charges the price of twelve, the output sold (which will be determined by demand) will be ten. In other words she cannot charge the price of twelve and plan on selling twenty units. In order for her to sell twenty units, the price has to be lower because of the nature of the demand curve.

The following table shows revenue, cost, and profit situations when ten units of output are sold.

PRICE	QUANTITY	TR = PxQ	TC = TCxQ	PROFIT = TR-TC OR (P-ATC)Q
$12	10	$12x10=120	$6x10 = $60	$120-$60 = $60 (P-ATC)Q=($12-$6)x$10 = 60

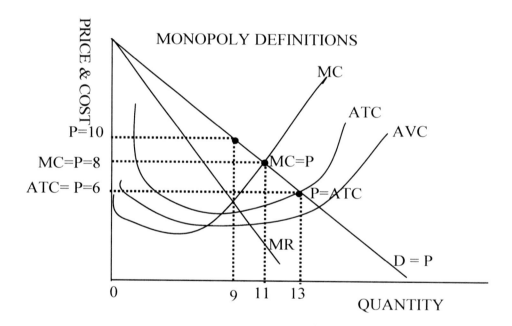

A monopolist, whose cost and revenue structures are depicted above, will produce 9 units and charge a price of $10. The quantity of nine is called monopoly output and the price of twelve is monopoly price. This is determined by equating marginal cost and marginal revenue. A monopolist will not, either willingly or knowingly, charge a price other than $10. If she was forced to charge according to the marginal cost (P = MC), the price would be $8 and the output 11.The price of $8 is called a marginal cost price and the output of 11 is a socially desirable output. Why is it a socially desirable output? The price of $6 is called a Full Cost Price or average cost pricing (P =ATC). The firm will break-even and earn a normal return at the price of $6.

COMPARED TO PERFECT COMPETITION
A MONOPOLIST RESTRICTS OUTPUT
AND CHARGES A HIGHER PRICE

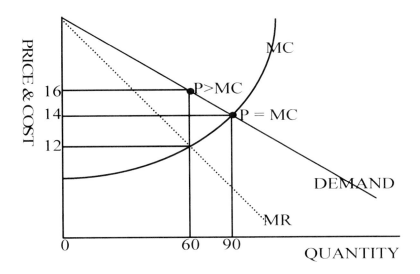

A rational monopolist will maximize profits by producing a monopoly output of 60 units where MC = MR and charge a monopoly price of $16. If she were to behave like a competitive firm and produce where MC = P, she would produce 90 units of output and charge a price of $14 which, by definition, will be a 'fair' price and lead to a socially desirable output. It follows then that a monopolist restricts output and charges a higher price. Another way of showing these monopoly inefficiencies is to imagine a competitive industry that is taken over by a single producer who, after consolidation, behaves like a monopolist. We predict that after the take over, output will be reduced and price will rise. The diagrams below demonstrate this point.

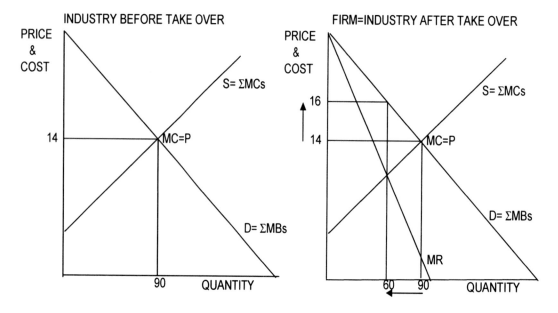

Before the industry was taken over by a monopolist, it was producing 90 units of output and the market price was $14. After the take over, the monopolist behaves as expected and derives a marginal revenue curve and equates marginal revenue to marginal cost in order to maximize profits. In so doing she produces 60 units of output and charges the price of $14. The price rises and output falls and ends up charging a price that is higher than marginal cost as we predicted.

You will recall that in a competitive market equilibrium is reached when price is equal to marginal cost. The consumers and producers maximize their gains at that point. Any other price reduces these gains and leaves either the consumers or the producers dissatisfied. Monopoly inefficiencies are discussed in greater detail in chapter ten.

HOMEWORK ON MONOPOLY

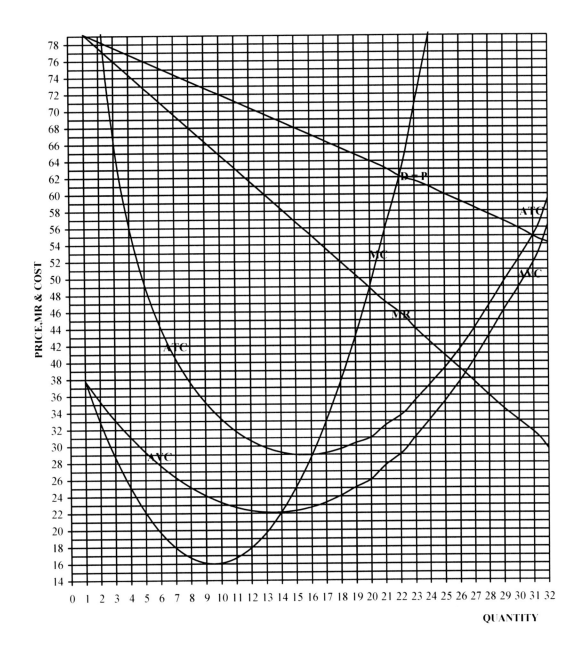

Use the graph above depicting the revenue and cost structures of
a **profit-maximizing monopolist** to answer the following questions:
a) What output will she produce and sell?
b) What price will she charge?
c) What will her total costs be?
d) What will her total revenue be?
e) Compute her total profits

f) What is the monopoly price?
g) What is the monopoly output?
h) What is the price that would lead to economic efficiency?
i) What would the output be if economic efficiency was achieved?
j) What is the full cost price?
k) Compute total variable costs (TVC)
l) Compute total fixed costs (TFC)

OUTPUT	TR	PRICE	MR	MC	PROFIT	TC
1	34.68					38.10
2	68.72					62.80
3	102.12					84.70
4	134.88					104.40
5	167.00					122.50
6	198.48					139.60
7	229.32					156.30
8	259.52					173.20
9	289.08					190.90
10	318.00					210.00
11	346.28					231.10
12	373.92					254.80
13	400.92					281.70
14	427.28					312.40
15	453.00					347.50

2) i) Complete the columns for price, MR, and MC for a profit maximizing
   monopolist whose cost and revenue structures are depicted in the above
   table.

   ii) a) What output will the firm produce and sell?
      b) What price will the firm charge?
      c) How much profit (total profit) will the firm get?
      d) At what level of output and price would economic
         efficiency be achieved? (Assuming the monopolist is
         forced to produce an **efficient** level of output?

CHAPTER 8: MONOPOLISTIC COMPETITION

Monopolistic competition has, as the expression indicates, both the elements of perfect competition and monopoly. It is a market structure between the extreme cases of perfect competition and monopoly. A monopolistically competitive market has many firms selling similar but not identical products.

The product sold by a firm is differentiated from other products. Examples of firms in a monopolistically competitive market are retail stores, restaurants, gasoline stations, convenience stores, and drug stores.

Unlike perfect competition and monopoly, the firm uses price and non-price competition. Price competition as you can imagine, has limitations because if you lower price in the inelastic range of your demand curve you will lose revenue. In any case you cannot lower price below your average total cost. The tool most used to compete and survive, is non-price competition. This involves measures that try, as much as possible, to differentiate one firm's product from another firm's product. If this succeeds, the firm in fact acquires market power over its product. Market power is the ability to control price.

The firm faces competition but it has some degree of market power because of product differentiation and therefore faces a downward sloping demand curve for its product. In the long run these tools of non-price competition (product differentiation) may actually increase demand (shift the demand curve outward) and make demand inelastic. Note: the expressions 'tools of product differentiation' and 'non-price competition' are used interchangeably in this book.

TOOLS OF NON-PRICE COMPETITION
Quality
A firm that makes a good quality product will inevitably have an advantage over its competition. Quality may depend on perceived physical appearance, material used, or design. It may be real or perceived, but as long as consumers are convinced that a product is of good quality, a firm will come out ahead.

Trade marks and brand names
Trademarks and brand names serve the function of identifying the product and reinforcing the uniqueness and hence quality of the product. A brand name product will sell at a relatively higher price because of the perception that the product is a high quality product and it is associated with certain good attributes. This is the reason why firms will fight tooth and nail to protect their trademarks and brand names.

Guarantees and warrants
Guarantees and warrants also try to make a statement about the quality of a product. The firms are saying that we stand by our product because it is of good quality. Imagine the cost that would be involved if a firm guaranteed a shoddy product and hundreds of people were frequently being compensated because the product was defective.

Packaging

A nicely packaged product may attract the attention of the consumer and consumers will prefer a product that cannot be easily tempered with. All these may make the product attractive.

Convenience

Some firms provide convenience to their customers by opening for extended hours, home delivery, and home services.

Advertising

Informative advertising tries to give information on things like price, location, and the hours the business is open and generally tries make consumers aware that the product exists. Persuasive advertising will help in product differentiation by extolling the product and its attributes. Advertising can also help establish brand names. Establishing brand names is a powerful tool of product differentiation because some consumers look at the brand name and immediately associate it with quality. In the end, advertising may increase market share, increase market power, and act as a barrier to entry. A firm in a perfect competitive market is not going to advertise because it can sell any output it wants at the going price. A monopolist is not likely to advertise because she has all the market to herself.

LONG RUN SITUATIONS OF FIRMS IN MONOPOLISTIC COMPETITION.

In the long run most firms will earn a normal return because of easy entry but some firms will still earn abnormal profits because of successful product differentiation.

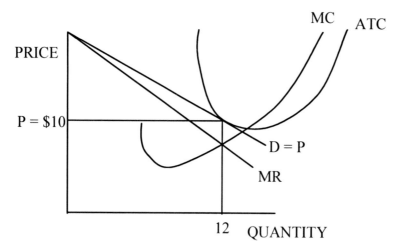

Most firms will earn a normal return in the long run
P = ATC

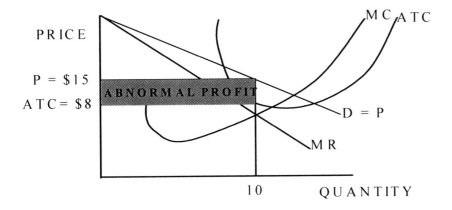

PRICE

P = $15

ATC = $8

ABNORMAL PROFIT

MC ATC

D = P

MR

10   QUANTITY

Some firms will earn an abnormal return in
the long run. P > ATC

Let us compare the characteristics of monopolistic competition to those of perfect
competition and monopoly. This should give us an opportunity to review the distinguishing
characteristics and outcomes of the two market structures we studied earlier.

PERFECT COMPETITION	MONOPOLISTIC COMPETITION	MONOPOLY
There are very many sellers	There are many sellers	There is a single seller
The products are perfect substitutes (homogeneous products)	The products are close substitutes (similar but not identical products)	The product has no close substitutes
There are no barriers to entry and exit	There are no barriers to entry and exit	There are barriers to entry and exit
Has no market power	Has some market power	Has market power
A firm in the industry faces a perfectly elastic demand curve for its product **(see graph below)**	A firm faces a downward sloping elastic demand curve for its product	A firm faces a downward sloping inelastic demand curve for its product
Does not use price competition	Uses price competition	Does not use price competition
Does not use tools of non-price competition	Uses the tools of non-price competition	Does not use tools of non-price competition
To survive in the long run, the firm produces at the lowest costs	To survive in the long run the firm, uses non-price competition	To survive in the long run, the firm must have barriers to entry, especially economies of scale.
The firm achieves economic efficiency	The firm does not achieve economic efficiency	The firm does not achieve economic efficiency
In the long run the firm achieves technical efficiency	The firm does not achieve technical efficiency	The firm does not achieve technical efficiency

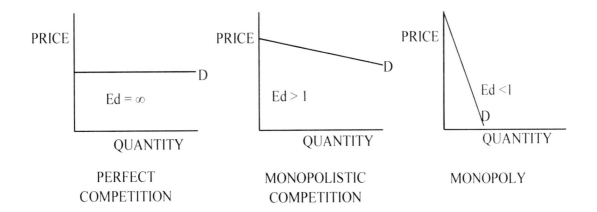

PERFECT
COMPETITION

MONOPOLISTIC
COMPETITION

MONOPOLY

CHAPTER 9: OLIGOPOLY

Oligopoly is a market structure in which few firms dominate the market. In terms of the number of firms, oligopoly lies between monopolistic competition and monopoly.

CHARACTERISTICS OF OLIGOPOLY:
1) There are few firms in the industry (3 to 10)
   We start from three because an industry with two firms is called a duopoly.
2) Some firms sell homogeneous products like cement, copper, zinc, and aluminum while most firms sell differentiated products like cars, instant breakfast, car rentals, tires, cigarettes, and disposable diapers.
3) There are barriers to entry, which may take the form of patents, control of inputs, and technological superiority
4) Firms depend on price and non-price competition
5) There is mutual interdependence between firms.

Firms in this type of market survive in the long run because of economies of scale and product differentiation

Since there are few firms, the industry is characterized by mutual interdependence. The actions of one firm may affect the profitability and survival of other firms in the industry and as such each firm tries to watch, and if necessary, react to the behavior of its rivals. Their actions therefore tend to be interdependent. Interdependent actions may take the form of price competition, guarantees, low cost financing and service contracts. As for price competition, firm **A** may start by reducing its price say by 10% and firm **B** may react by reducing its price by 15%. If firm **A** counters by reducing price by 20%, then it becomes a price war, which may lead to self-destruction.

There is no single model that can be used to analyze output determination and profit maximization, the same way we did in the cases of perfect competition, monopolistic competition and monopoly because of the mutual interdependence outlined above.

Oligopoly power is determined by market share and it is measured by concentration ratios. A concentration ratio is the percentage of industry sales or output accounted for by four or eight firms. Four-firm concentration ratios of 80% would indicate a high degree of oligopoly power. The problems with concentration ratios are that they ignore imported products and do ignore the size of the rest of the firms and therefore competition in the industry. If the firms excluded in the computation of the concentration ratio a large in size, then the big four or the big eight cannot dominate them. On the other hand, if the excluded firms are many and small, the big firms will dominate them to the disadvantage of the consumers.

The index currently popular with the Justice Department for antitrust enforcement is the Herfindahl-Hirsschman Index (HHI). The Herfindahl-Hirsschman Index is the sum of the squares of the market shares of all the firms in the industry. The more firms there are in an industry the smaller the index will be. In other words, if an industry is less concentrated, the HHI will be lower.

A monopoly with 100% market share will have a HHI of $100^2 = 10,000$.

A duopoly where each firm has 60% and 40% market share respectively, will have an index of $60^2 + 40^2 = 3600 + 1600 = 5,200$. Ten firms with equal market shares of 10%, will have an HHI of $10^2 + 10^2 + 10^2 + 10^2 + 10^2 + 10^2 + 10^2 + 10^2 + 10^2 + 10^2 = 1,000$. The advantage of the HHI is that it takes into account more firms in the industry.

CONCENTRATION RATIONS OF 4 AND 8 LARGEST MANUFACTURING COMPANIES AND THE HHI INDEXES OF 50 LARGEST COMPANIES IN THE UNITED STATES

INDUSTRY GROUP AND INDUSTRY	VALUE SHIPMENT ($1000)	PERCENT OF VALUE SHIPMENTS ACCOUNTED FOR BY THE LARGEST COMPANIES		HHI INDEX FOR 50 LARGEST COMPANIES
		4 LARGEST COMPANIES	8 LARGEST COMPANIES	
Breakfast cereal	9,098,833	82.9	93.5	2445.9
Breweries	18,203,492	89.7	93.4	D
Tobacco	3,6075,313	83.4	93.3	D
Alkalies & chlorine	2,465,183	79.7	92.3	2870.1
Resilient floor covering	1,684,216	86.9	98.9	2983.5
Tire mfg (except retreading)	14,728,525	72.4	90.8	1690.3
Glass container	4,198,122	91.1	98.0	2959.9
Primary smelting and refining copper	6,128,170	94.5	D	2392.3
Small arms ammunition	976,944	88.9	93.8	D
Photographic and photocopying equipment	8,290,986	80.9	85.0	D
Electric lamp bulb and parts	3,306,009	88.9	94.3	2849
Automobile and light duty motor vehicles	205,543,825	88.3	97.5	2862.8
Automobiles	95,365,667	79.5	96.3	2349.7
Light trucks and utility vehicles	110,178,158	99.3	99.9	D
Heavy duty trucks	14,509,032	74.4	90.3	1597.1
Source: U.S. Census Bureau, 1997 Economic Census. The 'D', according to the bureau, means the data was withheld to avoid disclosing data of individual companies.				

SOLUTIONS TO THE SELF-DESTRUCTIVE BEHAVIOR OF OLIGOPOLY

Sometimes the firms and the government may undertake certain measures to prevent the self-destructive behavior of cutthroat competition because in some instances intense competition may not be in the interest of the companies involved and the consumers.

OPEN COLLUSION: CARTELS

Open collusion may take the form of a cartel. The most famous example of a cartel is the Organization of the Petroleum Producing Countries (OPEC).
The idea of a cartel is to bring firms together to jointly determine output and pricing policies thus behaving like a monopoly. The scheme will succeed if the firms are few and there is no cheating. Cartels are illegal in the U.S. unless sanctioned by government authorities like in the case of milk cartels.

TACIT COLLUSION: PRICE LEADERSHIP

There are three types of price leaderships namely, dominant-firm price leadership, collusive price leadership, and barometric price leadership.

Dominant-Firm Leadership.

In this case a firm with the largest market share sets price and others follow. The firm in this case has overwhelming cost advantages and the rest of the firms have no choice but to follow the leader. The problem, for small firms, is that the price set by the leader may be below cost for some firms and it may not be high enough to guarantee abnormal profits for others. If, on the other hand, a dominant firm sets a price that is too high, new firms may enter the industry and old firms may expand thus eventually reducing the dominant firm's market share. U.S. steel and IBM's market shares decreased this way. Examples of firms that have played a key role in price leadership in their respective industries are; U.S. steel in the steel industry, R .J. Reynolds in the cigarette industry, Firestone in the automobile tire industry, Alcoa in the aluminum industry, IBM in the computer industry, and Xerox in the photocopier industry.

Collusive Price Leadership

In the case of collusive price leadership, a few large firms set price and expect other firms to follow. The scheme will not work if the big firms have no power to discipline other firms to tow the line by adhering to the pricing policies set by the bigger firms.

Barometric Price Leadership

In this case the firm that has more information on changing cost and demand conditions in the industry, will act as a leader. It could be a small firm with no power to discipline other firms, but other firms will follow the leader as long as the price reflects true market conditions.

CHAPTER 10: THE CAUSES OF MARKET IMPERFECTIONS AND THE ROLE OF GOVERNMENT

The market system, we discussed earlier, has a lot of desirable outcomes and it is well suited to address the basic economic problem. The problem, however, is that in some cases the market fails to lead to desirable and efficient economic outcomes thus making the role of government necessary. The market fails to lead to efficient economic outcomes whenever monopolies, externalities, public goods, and asymmetrical information are involved. The market may perform efficiently according to the assumptions and conditions we have outlined, but lead to a distribution of income where some people are so poor as to meet the basic needs of housing, clothing and shelter.

CAUSES OF MARKET IMPERFECTIONS: MONOPOLY

In chapter 12 we showed how a monopoly under allocates society's resources. In this section we shall use the concepts of consumer surplus and producer surplus as another approach for discussing monopoly inefficiencies. Later we shall discuss the problems associated with a particular type of monopoly called a natural monopoly.

Consumer surplus is the difference between what a consumer is willing to pay and what she actually pays for the product. If the market price of a gallon of milk is $2.30 and a consumer's marginal utility was $5, then the consumer would actually be willing pay $5 for the gallon of milk. Her surplus in this case is $2.70. Consumer surplus is measured by the area between the demand curve and price on the demand diagram (see the diagram below). Producer surplus is the difference between price and marginal cost or the difference between total revenue and total variable cost. It is measured by the area between the marginal cost curve and price or the supply curve and price (see the diagram below). Note that producer surplus is not the same thing is profit when there are fixed costs. Producer surplus (PS) = Total Revenue (TR) - {Total Cost (TC) - Total Fixed Cost (TFC)}. Producer Surplus = Profits + TFC.

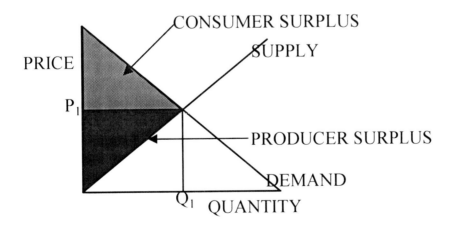

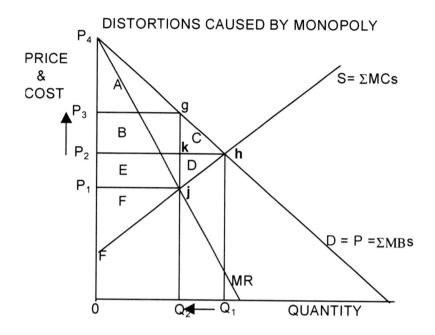

DISTORTIONS CAUSED BY MONOPOLY

When supply is equal to demand all possible gains from trade, in form of consumer and producer surpluses are realized. In the above diagram consumer surplus is represented by area P_4hP_2 (A + B + C) and producer surplus is represented by P_2hF (E + D + F). These gains from trade will be realized under perfect competition but a monopolist will reduce these gains from exchange when she takes over and operates as a monopolist and maximize profits at the level of output where marginal cost is equal to marginal revenue.

If a monopoly takes over, the gains from trade are less than before by area ghj (i.e. C + D). Now total surplus is A + B + E + F. The new consumer surplus is A and the new producer surplus is B + E + F. In the process, consumers have lost areas B + C and producers have lost area D but gained B. The difference between old total surplus and the new total surplus is

(A + B + C + D + E + F) - (A + B + E + F) = C + D. Area ghj (C + D)

measures the social loss (social cost or welfare loss or deadweight loss) caused by a monopoly. Even if a monopolist was taxed by the amount of his gain (i.e. P_3gkP_2) and the proceeds redistributed to the consumers, the consumer gains would not be restored to their original level because area C will still be unaccounted for.

We have now seen that a monopolist restricts output and charges a relatively higher price and in so doing reduces the gains from trade. It is now clear why the government would be interested in regulating monopolies. Antitrust laws have been passed in the U.S. to promote competition by curbing behavior that restricts competition and by preventing firms from dominating the market. Some firms have been broken up, AT&T being an example.

NATURAL MONOPOLIES

A natural monopoly is a firm that serves the entire market more efficiently than two or more firms would. Examples of a natural monopoly are a gas station in a remote area, a corner grocery store, a convenience store, and public utilities. Some natural monopolies like public utilities are associated with falling average costs for big ranges of their output. An electric company for example once set up may not incur extra cost to supply an extra consumer.

Since some natural monopolies are inevitable but provide essential services, federal, state, and local governments try to regulate them. The history and details of business government regulation are discussed in the Economics of Industrial Organization (Industrial Organization) course. Here we shall discuss briefly the problems associated with regulating a natural monopoly.

THE DILEMMA OF REGULATING A NATURAL MONOPOLY

The dilemma is to determine a price which is both fair to the consumers and to the producers. Below is an outline of the various methods of regulation that have been attempted.

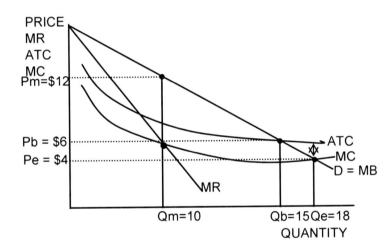

REGULATION METHODS:

Marginal Cost Pricing: The firm may be forced to charge a price equal to its marginal cost, i.e. $4 (in the above diagram) and therefore produce 18 units. At the output of 18, however, ATC is greater than price and the firm will incur a loss. The government may then be forced to subsidize it. The firm cannot do research and development at marginal cost price.

Average Cost Pricing (or Full Cost Pricing):

With average cost pricing, a firm is made to charge according to its average total costs. In this case the firm will charge $6 and produce 15 units. The firm merely breaks even and earns a normal return on its investment. Again there are few opportunities for research, reinvestment, and development.

Incentive Regulation:

What incentive regulation does is to set a price above ATC but below monopoly price (Pm) and guarantee the price for a number of years. The price cannot be revised upwards or downwards. If costs rise, profits will fall and therefore the firm may be induced to cut costs. If it does, then it will enjoy abnormal profits. For some firms, however, inefficiency may be encouraged because the rate is guaranteed. Remember this is not a contestable market. If the rate allowed is too low, there may be less reinvestment and expansion. A regulated price may be too low if demand is wrongly estimated.

A Two-Part Tariff:

A two-part tariff means that a consumer pays a set price (fixed price) for services, and then charged according to usage. Examples of these would be the basic charges for utilities, and cover charges in a social club. The idea is to help the consumer avail her self to a necessary service and at the same time help the business make a profit by charging according to marginal cost.

If the monopoly price of $12 was allowed, then the government may have to subsidize consumers because many consumers may be priced out of an essential product or service.

CAUSES OF MARKET IMPERFECTIONS: EXTERNALITIES

Externalities or spillovers exist when a production or consumption activity has an indirect effect on other production or consumption activities that is not reflected in market prices. This means that the costs of producing or the benefit of consuming a product or service spill over to those who do not produce or consume the product.

There are two types of externalities namely, a negative externality and a positive externality. With negative externality somebody imposes a cost (harm) to somebody else who is not directly involved in producing or consuming the product. In this case the price of the product does not reflect social value i.e. Marginal Social Cost (MC) diverges from Marginal Private Cost (MPC). If a student plays loud music in a dormitory room, her enjoyment may negatively affect her roommates by, for example, interfering with their sleep, their studies and so on. This would be an example of a negative externality.

A factory that pollutes a river or a lake may cause the destruction of marine life and reduce the quality of water. This is a cost imposed on the people in the surrounding area who depend on the lake for their livelihood. When an oil refinery pollutes the air with smoke, the residents bear spill over costs for which they are not compensated.

MARKET IMPERFECTIONS AND NEGATIVE EXTERNALITIES

Let us focus on pollution as an example of a negative externality and the inefficiencies that it causes. A factory, which pollutes a river that drains into a lake and affects the livelihood and health of the neighborhood community, creates a negative externality. The factory takes into account its internal cost and demand structures and produces a level of output where marginal private cost is equal to marginal private benefit (MPC = MPB). The expression private cost means that the producer considers her internal costs and does not take into account the external costs imposed by a negative externality. The marginal private cost, therefore, is not a 'true' cost if a negative externality is involved. In order to reflect the true cost, the external cost must be added to the private cost.

True cost is: Marginal Private Cost (MPC) + External Cost (MEC) = Marginal Social Cost (MC). This is the essence of saying that a negative externality causes a divergence between MPC and MSC since MPC is less than MSC. It follows therefore that the price charged is less than marginal social cost and as such there is over allocation of society's resources. Note that if there was no externality, MPC would be the same thing as MSC. The following graph demonstrates the relationships discussed above.

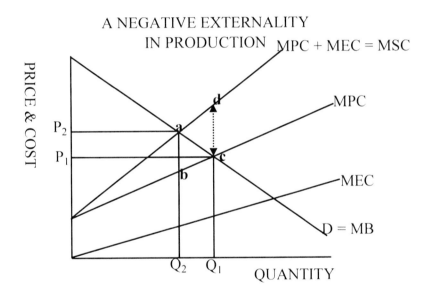

The firm will produce Q_1 where MPC = MB but in so doing it ignores the MEC. Ideally it should produce Q_2 where MSC = MB thereby taking into account the marginal external cost. For any output greater than Q_2, the social cost is the difference between MSC and MB (the demand curve). The social cost of this particular externality is triangle **adc**. The industry over allocates at Q_1 since MC is greater than MB.

CORRECTING NEGATIVE EXTERNALITIES

Our previous discussion has shown that whenever externalities are involved, competitive markets fail to produce an efficient level of output thus reducing the consumers' welfare. This then calls for some intervention to correct these negative outcomes.

The methods we about to discuss are both government solutions and private solutions but government solutions are emphasized.

I. THE PIGOUVIAN TAX (OR A PER-UNIT TAX):

The Pigouvian tax, first proposed by the British economist A.C. Pigou, is a tax that is levied on every unit of output that is produced. It is suggested that in the case of a negative externality, a tax equal to the external cost caused by pollution at the efficient level of output (Q_2) be imposed. The amount of the tax is therefore the distance **ab** shown in the following graph titled 'A Pigouvian Tax'. The distance **ab** is equal to the amount of the marginal external cost (marginal damage) at Q_2 (efficient level of output). The amount of the tax **t** is equal to **ab**. Note that at Q_2, MPC + MEC = **ab**. A per-unit tax in the amount of **t** will increases the effective marginal cost as each output is now supplied at a higher cost (i.e. MPC + TAX). This leads to a parallel shift of the MPC function to the MPC + TAX function and in order to maximize profits, Q_2 must be produced. Q_2 happens to be the efficient level of output given that MSC is equal to MB at Q_2. The tax has thus forced the firm to take care of the externality and produce a socially desirable output.

The main assumption in all this is that the damage caused by the firm is an increasing function of the output produced. If you increase output, you will increase the damage and vice versa. In this case the damage is decreased by the tax. The externality in this case is internalized because the producers are made to add the marginal external cost to the their marginal private cost thus taking into account actual social cost of their decisions. Note, however, that the damage that is caused by pollution for example is not necessarily eliminated. The key point is that an efficient level of output is produced. People who are directly affected by the damage will have the damage reduced. The tax revenues resulting from the tax is area P_2P***ba**. Note that compensation for the victims of pollution is note necessary to achieve economic efficiency.

The problem with a corrective tax, however, is that the quantity produced decreases and the price of the product goes up. Consumers not directly affected by the externality will be unhappy. Another problem is that it is difficult to estimate the monetary value of the marginal external cost and marginal benefit. If the MEC is wrongly estimated, an incorrect tax may be imposed thus leading to inefficient outcomes. The estimation is also complicated by the fact that the sources of an externality may be difficult to identify. In an industrial area with many firms, for example, it may be difficult to identify the polluters and determine how much pollution they emit. Another problem is that if MPC falls after the imposition of a tax, a firm may produce more and pollute more.

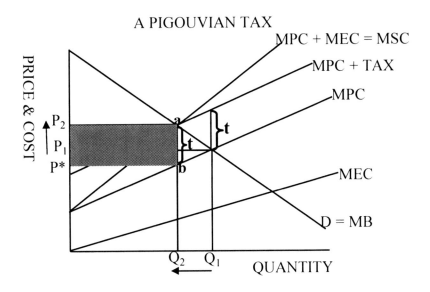

A PIGOUVIAN TAX

II. THE PIGOUVIAN SUBSIDY (OR PER-UNIT SUBSIDY):

The Pigouvian subsidy works much like the per-unit tax in that it raises the producers' effective costs. In this case a polluter is paid not to pollute. In the following graph, a subsidy of **s** is paid so that the producer produces Q_2 instead of Q_1. If the producer decides to produce Q_1, she forgoes **s** and this may not be in her interest. We can therefore consider **s** as an opportunity cost. The perceived total cost is therefore MPC + **s**. At Q_1 cost exceeds benefit (price) by **s**. For any output greater than Q_2 cost will be grater than benefit and it will be in the interest of the producer to produce the efficient output of Q_2.

It looks strange that somebody would in effect be bribed not to pollute instead of making her legally liable. This may be justified on the grounds that an increase in the cost of production may force marginal firms to shut down and lead to a fall in output and employment.

The problems of estimation, identification, reduction in quantity, and the increase in price associated with a per-unit tax are also applicable here. Another problem is that other economic activities are taxed to pay for the subsidy, which leads to market distortions and negative effects on incentives. Subsidies may cause a problem by attracting new firms, which may lead to more pollution.

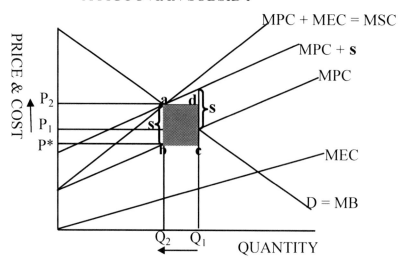

A PIGOUVIAN SUBSIDY

III. EMISSION TAXES:

Instead of taxing the output produced, the firms are taxed according to quantity of pollution they produce. The advantage of this method over the unit taxes is that firms can develop new technology to reduce pollution instead of reducing output.

IV. AUCTIONING POLLUTION PERMITS (TRADABLE PERMITS):

In this case the market is used to reduce pollution instead of the government. Business firms are issued permits by the government to emit a limited amount of pollutants in the environment. The permits act as an incentive for companies to reduce pollution because they are tradable. Businesses can take the advantage of this by lowering their pollution levels. The problem with this approach is that big firms will have an advantage over the small firms because, given their resources, they are likely to adopt the cheapest ways of reducing pollution. This will enable the bigger firms to sell their permits and become even bigger.

V. THE COASE THEOREM:

In 1960 Professor Ronald Coase, of the university of Chicago, published a very important article titled Problems of Social Cost. Coase was concerned with the inefficiencies of taxes and government regulation in general. He argued, in his paper, that if property rights are well defined and transactions costs are low, individuals will bargain and trade and eventually rich an efficient outcome without government intervention. Note that externalities exist because property rights are not well defined. Specific individuals do not own the air, lakes, rivers, parks, for example and as such property rights are not well defined. If they were privately owned then the problem of externalities would not arise.

Coase contended that it may be in the interest of an aggrieved party to bribe the causer of a negative externality to reduce or stop the externality. Let us say Jeremy was the polluter and David was the victim of Jeremy's pollution. If the property rights are assigned to Jeremy, David can bribe (pay) Jeremy not to pollute. The question is how much bribe will David be willing to pay and whether Jeremy will accept any payment.

The size of the bribe Jeremy must receive in order not to pollute must be greater than the net benefit Jeremy derives from his production activity.

Let **b** = bribe. MB = marginal benefit, MPC = marginal private cost, MD = marginal damage. The size of the bribe must be: **b>(MB-MPC)**

i.e. b >net benefits. David will be willing to pay a bribe that is less or equal to the marginal damage caused by pollution. David's payment will be: **b≤MD.**

The bribe (b) cannot be greater than the marginal damage.

As long as the amount that David is willing to pay Jeremy exceeds the opportunity cost to Jeremy for not polluting, then the opportunity for bargain exists. The requirement for bargain is : MD >(MB - MPC). The perceived marginal damage must be greater than net benefits. If MD is less than marginal benefits, then there is no room for bargain.

LIMITATIONS OF THE COASE THEOREM

The Coase theorem is not likely to work if the number of economic agents involved is big. In this case the costs of organizing, bargaining and enforcement will be very high. That is why sometimes you have class action suits. There is also the problem of identifying the sources of an externality. If the source cannot be clearly determined there cannot be bargaining and enforcement. It is also difficult to measure the damage accurately to determine the amount of the bribe. Since we cannot assign property rights for air, lakes, rivers and oceans, the theorem cannot work. Lastly the theorem will not work if transactions costs are very high.

VI. SUBSIDIES: The government can provide incentives for firms not to pollute by giving subsidies to encourage the introduction of new technology as is done in Japan. This may be superior to regulation because in regulation, producers may produce too much or too little if polluters with different marginal benefits and marginal private costs are forced to reduce pollution by the same amount.

A NEGATIVE EXTERNALITY IN CONSUMPTION

Second hand smoke, for example, is deemed harmful to people who are exposed to it. In other words smokers, through their consumption activity, impose damage to non-smokers. Smokers derive marginal private benefits from their consumption activity and these marginal benefits are depicted by the demand curve in the diagram below. Given the smokers' demand pattern and assuming that there is no externality in production, producers of cigarettes will produce a level of output Q_1, where marginal private benefits (MPB) are equal to marginal social cost (MSC) and charge a price equal to P_1. At Q_1, however, the marginal social benefit is smaller than the marginal private benefit MSB<MPB by the amount of the external cost imposed on non-smokers. In this case there is overproduction of cigarettes and society's resources are being over allocated. With no externality, output Q_2 would be produced and the market would set the price of P_2. Output Q_2 is the socially desirable output and society would be better off by reducing production from Q_1 to Q_2.

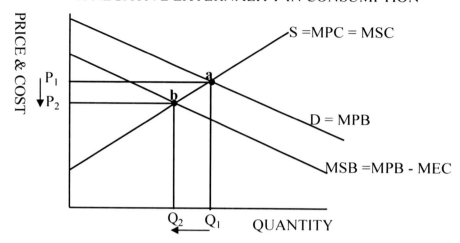

A NEGATIVE EXTERNALITY IN CONSUMPTION

PRICE & COST

P_1
P_2

S =MPC = MSC

a

b

D = MPB

MSB =MPB - MEC

Q_2 Q_1 QUANTITY

MARKET IMPERFECTIONS AND POSITIVE EXTERNALITIES

You have a positive externality when somebody creates a benefit to somebody else, but the creator of the benefit is not compensated for her services. The benefits spill over to somebody who is not involved in producing or consuming the product. In this case Marginal Social Benefit (MSB) diverges from Marginal Private Benefit (MPB). People in a neighborhood who cut their loans and paint their houses may create benefits for the rest of the community if property values go up. Of course those who neglect their properties may affect property values negatively thus imposing a negative externality. A person who shovels her sidewalk creates a benefit to those who walk on it. A scientist who through research discovers a cure for a disease creates a positive externality. An inventor who invents a machine that improves methods of production across industries also creates a positive externality. Somebody, who spends money on education and acquires useful skills, creates a positive externality to society.

In the case of a positive externality, as we have observed, MSB diverges from MPB. In the following graph MSB = marginal social benefits,
MPB = marginal private benefits, MEB = marginal external benefit,
MSC= marginal social cost. When we look at the graph below, we can see that a scientist involved in research , for example, will produce where MPB = MSC i.e. output = Q_1. At that point MSB is greater than MPB and MSC because the scientist causes a positive externality. This means that she under allocates society's resources by producing where marginal social benefit is greater than marginal social cost (MSB>MSC). To induce her to produce the efficient level of output of Q_2, a subsidy of **s** per unit must be paid, so that she produces where MSC = MSB. See the second diagram titled correcting a positive externality.

A POSITIVE EXTERNALITY IN PRODUCTION

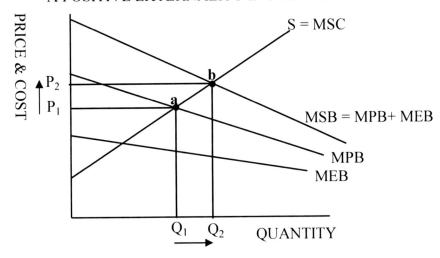

CORRECTING A POSITIVE EXTERNALITY

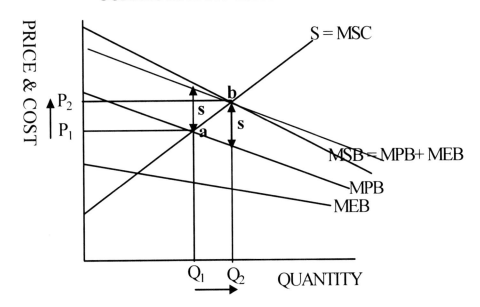

MARKET IMPERFECTIONS AND PUBLIC GOODS

Goods and services like a lighthouse, national parks, public television, public libraries, public education and highways are called public goods.

Public goods have two important characteristics.

1) Public goods are **non-rival in consumption** (i.e. they are non-depletable or non-exhaustible). Public goods are indivisible and the consumption of the good does not exhaust the product. This means that a person can benefit from the public good without reducing other people's consumption of it. Once produced, it can be supplied to an additional consumer at zero marginal cost. Compare this with a private good like a pen, a car, a TV or a computer. Private goods are rival in consumption. Once they have been consumed, another one must be made at an extra cost for another consumer who needs it.

2) Public goods are **non-exclusive**. Once they have been produced it may be very difficult to exclude consumers. This may create a free rider problem.

A free rider problem exists when people have an incentive to consume a product for which they do not pay. Let us say you are living with a roommate who does not care about the cleanliness of your apartment. If you care, the burden of making your apartment clean will fall on your shoulders. Other than the drastic action of kicking her out, you cannot exclude her from enjoying the benefit of your services. Your roommate in this case is a free rider. People in some local community may unanimously agree to increase educational and recreational services but when it comes to discussing the actual cost of these services, the unanimity breaks down. It breaks down because of the free rider problem.

EXAMPLES OF PUBLIC GOODS BY CATEGORY

1) EXCLUSIVE BUT NON-RIVAL IN CONSUMPTION (NON-DEPLETABLE):

A bridge is a good example of a product from which you can exclude consumers by charging a price but it is non-rival, especially during periods of low traffic. This is a semi-public good because it does not satisfy both characteristics. A television signal is also non-rival in consumption because one's consumption does not exhaust the product, and additional consumers can be supplied at zero marginal cost. It can, however, be exclusive if the signals are scrambled and a price is charged. Public parks, public swimming pools, roads, public libraries fall in this category but at some point they may be exhaustible. These are also called congestible public goods.

2) NON-EXCLUSIVE BUT RIVAL (DEPLETABLE):

Air may be non-exclusive but depletable if air pollution leads costs.

Fish in lakes and rivers is also non-exclusive but exhaustible because the more fish caught, the less fish available to others. Public high school education is non-exclusive but depletable because the more the students the more the desks, books, teachers that will be needed. Public high education will, therefore, be supplied at extra cost after a certain point.

3) EXCLUSIVE AND NON-RIVAL (PURE PUBLIC GOODS):

National defense, a lighthouse, Public television, public radio, environmental protection are examples of public goods that satisfy both characteristics. These are called pure public goods.

EFFICIENT PRODUCTION OF PUBLIC GOODS

We saw that a private good is supplied efficiently when its price is equal to its marginal cost. Since a public good is indivisible it is difficult to determine its marginal benefit or price. For a private good, marginal benefit is measured by the willingness to pay (i.e. price). For a public good, we must estimate individual marginal benefits and add them up vertically (i.e. get ($\sum$MB).

Note that we cannot just take one person's marginal benefit because the good is indivisible. To determine the efficient level of production we must then equate the sum of marginal benefits to marginal social cost . Efficient level of production implies:

($\sum$**MB = MSC).** The problem with this, however, is that the total marginal benefits may be underestimated or overestimated because consumers may not reveal their true preferences. Given the free rider problem, we expect consumers not to reveal correctly the amount they are willing to pay.

EFFICIENT PRODUCTION OF PUBLIC GOODS

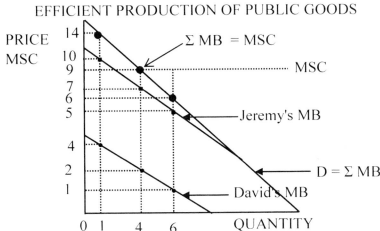

At Q=1, David's MB = 4 and Jeremy's MB = 10. This output would be inefficient because the sum of marginal benefits is greater than the sum of marginal social costs ($\sum$MB>MSC i.e. 14>9). At this level of output there would be under allocation of society's resources. At Q=4, David's MB=2 and Jeremy's MB=7. This would be an efficient level of output because the sum of marginal benefits is equal to marginal social cost ($\sum$MB=MSC i.e. 9=9).

At Q=6, David's MB=1 and Jeremy's MB=5.This level of output leads to over allocation of society's resources because the sum of marginal benefits is less than marginal social cost ($\sum$MB<MSC i.e. 6<9).

119

WHY DOES THE GOVERNMENT PRODUCE OR SUBSIDIZE THE PRODUCTION OF PUBLIC GOODS?

The government produces public goods because the private market fails to produce them and when the market does, it produces insufficient quantities. Most public goods like education, health care, nutrition, environmental and research programs provide positive externalities. Private markets may not produce public goods efficiently because of the lack of proper pricing. Consumers do not reveal their true preferences and a producer cannot estimate demand and a correct price to charge. The second reason is that exclusion costs may be very high.

Let us say that you start a business of constructing dams to prevent floods that devastate crops. Once the dam is constructed, you cannot exclude others from benefiting from the dam. You cannot selectively flood the fields of those who do not pay, for example. The exclusion costs in this case would be prohibitive and given the fact that you cannot charge a proper price for the services, the business will not be profitable. This problem of exclusion is made worse by the free-rider problem. The free-rider problem exists when people enjoy the benefits of a product without paying for it.

Difficulties in pricing and high exclusion costs imply that public goods may not be produced at all by the market. If produced, they may be over produced and therefore under consumed or may be under produced and therefore over consumed. The government may not supply efficient quantities of public goods, because pricing problems cannot be completely eliminated, but at least the government guarantees their production.

MARKET IMPERFECTIONS AND IMPERFECT INFORMATION

Perfect information, you will recall, is one of the most important conditions for efficient performance of competitive markets. Buyers must have equal access to information on product prices, product quality, and the location of the product. Sellers must know the prices, quality, and the availability of resources for meaningful competition to exist. Whenever there is a problem of information, markets will fail to perform efficiently. The problem of information can be divided into two categories namely costly information and asymmetric information.

ASYMMETRIC INFORMATION

In some cases there is inequality of information possessed by the parties in a transaction. In this case there is asymmetric information, which leads to market failure. The following are examples of the situations in which asymmetric information may arise.

ADVERSE SELECTION (DIFFERENTIAL RISK).

This problem can be found in the insurance industry and the banking industry. Lack of information leads to inability to distinguish between bad risk and good risk. An individual buying an insurance policy may not reveal all the pertinent information about herself. People who drive while drunk do not tell the insurance company that they are an accident waiting to happen and so are people who smoke and drink excessively and indulge in other bad health habits. As a result of this, an insurer cannot differentiate between bad risk and good risk and charge accordingly. Instead the insurer must charge a uniform rate for those who are a poor risk and those who are a good risk. The poor risk side of the market (buyers) has information that the other side of the market (sellers) does not have. The informed side of the market will self-select in such a way that they harm the uninformed side of the market. The bad risk category will mostly likely favor the average rate being charged and they are the most likely to be compensated for the losses. The good risk category on the other hand, will not like the rate and may prefer to withdraw from the market all together. Faced with this problem, insurance companies may decide not to offer insurance protection to certain groups of people like the elderly thereby leading to market failure.

The problem of adverse selection also exists in the banking industry. Small businesses, for example, are comprised of low-risk and high-risk categories. The high-risk category will present itself as low-risk and loan officers may not know all the relevant information to charge an interest rate commensurate with their high-risk ness. The bankers in this case face a dilemma of the appropriate rate to charge. If they charge too high a rate, good risk borrowers may withdraw from the loan market. If they charge a low rate, they will lose money. Faced with this dilemma, bankers may decide not to lend to small businesses thus leading to market failure.

MORAL HAZARD

The problem of moral hazard arises after a market transaction has been made. In the case of insurance, once people buy insurance, their behavior may change in such a way that insurance encourages the risk it is supposed to prevent. In other words, insurance may reduce incentive to reduce risk. Some people may take less care of themselves after they have insured themselves or they may visit doctors more frequently than is necessary. Drivers may not take proper precautions to avoid accidents, and homeowners may not take proper measures to avoid theft or fire. This may lead to higher premiums or insurers may decide not to offer insurance altogether. In the loanable funds markets, borrowers may undertake risky ventures after the loan has been secured. Again this may lead to higher interest rates and fewer loans. To take care of this nature of asymmetric information, financial intermediaries try to provide more information on borrowers and monitor their behavior.

THE LEMON PROBLEM

The lemon problem is another example of asymmetric information that is common in the used car market. The seller of a used car has more information about the condition of the car than the buyer. Let us suppose the market for used cars consists of good cars and bad cars (lemons). Since buyers may not distinguish between the good ones and the bad ones, they are likely to offer a price that is less than the equilibrium price. The sellers of good cars on the other hand will not be willing to sell at that price. As a result lemons will dominate the market. When the buyers realize this, they will even want to offer relatively lower prices and lemons will dominate even more. The sellers try to address this problem by signaling that their cars are good. They may offer limited warrants, money-back guarantees, free service contracts, or encourage the buyer to bring in a trusted mechanic to inspect the car.

THE PRINCIPLE-AGENT PROBLEM

The principle-agent problem occurs when an agent acts in her self-interest to the detriment of the principle's interests. An employer (the principle) hires an employee (the agent) to carry out certain tasks but the employee may not work hard or may spend time on activities that do not benefit the employer. It might be difficult to monitor the employee's performance and the result of this will be low productivity. If you higher a mechanic to repair your car, she may end up doing unnecessary repairs or inflating costs. Again it may be difficult to monitor these acts. The principle-agent problem could arise also when you are dealing with a lawyer, a doctor, a mortgage broker, or a building contractor.

INDEX

ABOUT THE AUTHOR:

Dr. Pirudas Lwamugira is Professor of economics at Fitchburg State College, Fitchburg Massachusetts. He teaches Principles of Microeconomics and Macroeconomics, Money and Banking, Public Finance, Industrial Organization, International Finance, and Econometrics at the undergraduate level. He also teaches corporate finance at the graduate level.

Dr. Lwamugira received a Bachelor of Arts degree from the University of East Africa, University College Dar es Salaam; an MBA degree in Banking and Finance from St. Joseph University in Philadelphia, and a Ph.D. in Economics from Temple University in Philadelphia.

Dr. Lwamugira has a varied experience in teaching economics to students of different backgrounds over thirty years. Before becoming tenured at Fitchburg State College, he had been a teacher at St. Thomas Moore's College, Ihungo, in Tanzania; a lecturer at Uganda College of Commerce; and had served as an adjunct economics faculty at Temple University and La Salle University in Philadelphia, and Rutgers University in Camden New Jersey.

CPSIA information can be obtained at www.ICGtesting.com
Printed in the USA
BVOW01s0908190714

359637BV00001B/2/A